THE FEMINIST PRESS

POR-TRAITS OF CHI-NESE WOM-EN IN REVO-LU-TION

by Agnes Smedley

*edited with an introduction
by Jan MacKinnon and Steve MacKinnon;
with an afterword by Florence Howe*

Library of Congress Cataloging in Publication Data:

Smedley, Agnes, 1890-1950
    Portraits of Chinese women in revolution.

    1. Women—China—History. 2. Smedley, Agnes, 1890-1950.
I. Title

HQ1737.S56 1976   301.41'2'0951   76-18896
ISBN 0-912670-44-4

Introduction copyright © 1976 by Jan MacKinnon and
Steve MacKinnon
Afterword copyright © 1976 by Florence Howe

With special acknowledgments to the Coordinating Council
of Literary Magazines for a grant that helped finance
the publication of this book, and to Frances Boehm,
Joan Kelly-Gadol, Amy Swerdlow, and Rose Rubin for their
kind assistance.

Grateful acknowledgment is made to:

Vanguard Press, Inc. and the estate of Agnes Smedley for
permission to reprint material from *China Fights Back* by Agnes
Smedley, copyright © 1938 by Vanguard Press, Inc.,
copyright © 1965 by Chu Teh; *China's Red Army Marches*
by Agnes Smedley, copyright © 1934, 1961 by Vanguard Press,
Inc.; *Chinese Destinies: Sketches of Present-Day China* by
Agnes Smedley, copyright © 1933, 1961 by Vanguard Press, Inc.

Alfred A. Knopf, Inc. and the estate of Agnes Smedley for
permission to reprint material from *Battle Hymn of China* by
Agnes Smedley, copyright © 1943, 1970 by Agnes Smedley.

Art Director/Designer: Susan Trowbridge

This book was typeset in Journal Roman by O.B.U., New York,
New York, with Souvenir and Hobo heads supplied by Nassau
Typographers, Plainview, New York. It was printed on 60 #
offset by R.R. Donnelley & Sons Company, Chicago, Illinois.

The photos used in the photographic portraits are
reproduced through the courtesy of Aino Taylor (page 192)
and the Arizona State University Archives (pages 194-203).
The cover illustration is by Joseph A. Smith.

First edition

*To friendship
between the peoples
of the
United States
and
The People's
Republic of China*

The Feminist Press offers alternatives in
education and in literature. Founded in 1970, this
nonprofit, tax-exempt educational and
publishing organization works to eliminate
sexual stereotypes in books and schools, providing
instead a new (or neglected) literature with
a broader vision of human potential. Our books—
high quality paperbacks—include reprints of
important works by women writers, feminist biographies
of women, and nonsexist children's books.
Curricular materials, bibliographies, directories,
and a newsletter provide information and
support for women's studies at every educational
level. Our Inservice projects help teachers develop
new methods to encourage students to become
their best and freest selves. Through our publications
and projects we can begin to recreate the forgotten
history of women, begin to create a more humane
and equitable society for the future. For a catalogue
of all our publications, please write to us.

TABLE OF CON- TENTS

INTRO-
DUC-
TION

By Jan MacKinnon
and Steve MacKinnon

With the reissue of her autobiographical novel, *Daughter of Earth* (The Feminist Press, 1973), and with the resurgence of American interest in China, Agnes Smedley (1892-1950) has become a vital voice to a new generation. To those who know her as a writer, a participant in revolutionary movements, and a vigorous feminist, Agnes Smedley has been an inspiration for their own struggles. She exposed prison conditions in

Portions of this introduction first appeared in "Agnes Smedley: A Working Introduction," *Bulletin of Concerned Asian Scholars*, 7, no. 1 (January-March 1975): 6-11. The editors wish to give special thanks to Paul Lauter and Marcela Lozano for their help and to Arizona State University's Faculty Grants Committee for financial assistance.

the United States; worked to establish birth control clinics in Germany, India, and China; raised funds and helped organize the Indian revolutionary movement against the British; defended Chinese writers against persecution by Chiang Kai-shek; became a war correspondent of international stature; raised funds for Chinese war relief; nursed wounded guerillas of the Chinese Red Army; and at the end of her life fought McCarthyism in the United States. What Agnes Smedley wrote and experienced now emerges with new importance to others working for self-determination and a new social order.

Smedley's activism and her feminism grew out of her personal and class background. Born into the rural poverty of northern Missouri, Smedley moved as a child through the shacks of many poor western towns and mining camps. Her father, hard-drinking, disappointed, and illiterate, maintained a flair for storytelling—at least until his spirit was broken while he was a coal miner in the Rockefellers' Trinidad, Colorado, mines. Chained by children and overwork, her mother took in laundry until she died in her late thirties of malnutrition, exposure, and exhaustion. Reared on the romantic tales of Jesse James, on cowboy ballads, and on the economic realities which forced her to be hired out as a domestic at age twelve, Smedley was stamped by the fervent individualism of the Old West, and by a keen understanding of what making a living meant—especially for a woman. The family depended on a prostitute aunt to keep it from total destitution, a relationship of which Smedley was both proud and ashamed all her life. (One of her last interests before she died was a study of prostitution in England.) Fear of the degradation lower-class women encountered in the endless cycle of sex, childbearing, and child rearing, made concrete in the lives of her mother and aunt, haunted and motivated Smedley throughout her life.

Her mother instilled another dream, ever-present in the experience of working people: that of liberating herself through education. Rich local materials in the Southwest indicate that Smedley's *Daughter of Earth* accurately portrays the bitterness she encountered trying to realize this dream. Aside from the grammar schools she sporadically attended during her family's periods of stability, Tempe Normal School (now Arizona State University) provided in 1911-12 her first significant educational experience. She became editor of the school paper. Many of her well-written stories of this period are obviously autobiographical; some re-emerged eighteen years later in *Daughter of Earth*. In Tempe, Smedley met her first husband, Ernest Brundin, and his sister, Thorburg. Both influenced her profoundly, although, as she wrote in the novel, her fears of sex and pregnancy, and the emotional agony of abortion, could lead only to divorce. At Tempe and later at San Diego State University (then San Diego Normal School) she advanced her education sufficiently to obtain a position teaching typing at the latter in 1914. She lost this position two years later because of her association with the Socialist party and with people who had been involved in San Diego's free speech movement of 1912, and possibly because of contacts with Indian nationalists. Jobless and seeking to deepen her political education, Smedley decided to move east to New York.

Her years in New York, 1917-20, reveal immense energy and commitment. While working as a secretary, she wrote for the Socialist party's newspaper, *The Call*, as well as for Margaret Sanger's *Birth Control Review*. She became more and more deeply involved with the Indian nationalist movement. During World War I, Indian nationalism was viewed by British and American authorities alike as a subversive movement, and its supporters in the United States as renegades, at best. British and United States intelligence operatives devel-

oped an intense interest in Smedley's activities, which
they were to pursue for over three decades and across
three continents. In March, 1918, Smedley and Salien-
dra Nath Ghose, a nationalist activist, were arrested in
New York. The Espionage Act indictment charged them
with stirring up rebellion against British rule in India
and with representing themselves as diplomats. Wartime
hysteria transformed the charge into part of a German
plot against our British allies. After six months in the
Tombs, Smedley was released on bail, raised in part by
Margaret Sanger, since Smedley had also been charged
with violating a local anti-birth-control law. In *The Call*,
Smedley published "Cell Mates," sketches of four
women prisoners with whom she did time. [1] Prison
deepened her radicalism and generated even greater
commitment to the Indian revolutionary movement.
Even with the indictment still pending—it was not
formally dropped until 1923—she edited a newsletter,
India News Service, acted as executive secretary of
Friends of Freedom for India, wrote, and raised
money. [2]

By 1920, the combined efforts of British intelligence
and the United States Department of Justice had largely
succeeded in suppressing the Indian revolutionary movement in the United States. Smedley's thinking had also
moved beyond the moderation of her earlier mentors,
like Lala Rajpat Rai (the fatherly professorial figure in
Daughter of Earth), toward a commitment to armed
revolution in India. For such reasons she decided to
move to Germany and to join a group called the Indian
Revolutionary Committee of Berlin. The last section of
Daughter of Earth, though set in the United States,
depicts her German period of intense activity and trial.

Berlin was the hub of the overseas Indian freedom
movement, and Smedley moved right at its center.
Emma Goldman described her and an Indian companion
in 1921:

She was a striking girl, an earnest and true rebel, who seemed to have no other interest in life except the cause of the oppressed people in India. Chat[t]o [her Hindu friend] was intellectual and witty, but he impressed me as a somewhat crafty individual. He called himself an anarchist, though it was evident that it was Hindu nationalism to which he had devoted himself entirely. [3]

The "crafty" fellow whom Goldman did not like was Virendranath Chattopadhaya, long the organizer of and intellectual force behind the Berlin group. He became Smedley's common-law husband as well as her mentor in further study of Marxist theory. Ultimately, however, her relationship with Chatto (as he was usually called) shattered her personal and political life. M.N. Roy's depiction of Smedley in the classic sexist stereotype of the temptress illustrates the hostility which her relationship with Chatto bred among other Indian revolutionaries:

. . . The famous revolutionary Chattopadhaya natural-ly commended himself for affection. She [Smedley] came over to Berlin and was known to have lived with Chattopadhaya for several years. It seems that she managed to poison Chatto's mind against me. In any case, she was the evil genius of the Indian revolution-ary group. . . . But for her influence, Chatto, who was an intelligent and practical man, would have behaved differently. I learned in the course of time that she was heartily disliked by all the other members of the group because of her pretension to be a more passion-ate Indian patriot than the Indians themselves. . . . [4]

In *Daughter of Earth* and to friends in the 1940s Smedley gave her side of the story: not only had she worked to provide financial support, but she had slavishly cooked and kept house for men who sat around talking about revolution at a distance. Moreover, other Indian revolutionaries recognized her positive contribution to the cause. Jawaharlal Nehru, for example, met Smedley in Berlin in 1926 and was sufficiently impressed to invite her to India after independence and to meet her in New York in 1949, more than twenty years later. Eventually, Smedley suffered a total nervous breakdown, for which writing *Daughter of Earth* was part of the therapy. Thereafter, while the personal and the political remained consciously meshed for her, Smedley would never again join a political organization nor become emotionally dependent on a man.

As had been the case in New York, Smedley's political involvements in Berlin and her educational pursuits extended beyond the Indian movement. She continued feminist activities, keeping in close personal touch with Margaret Sanger. She brought Sanger to Germany for a lecture tour in 1927, and was instrumental in opening Berlin's first birth control clinic in 1928. She also taught English and American studies at the University of Berlin, and persuaded the authorities there to accept her as a doctoral student in Indian history. She wrote numerous articles in German, some for academic journals, primarily on Indian history and on women.[5] She moved in the exciting intellectual circle of the German Left of the 1920s. Käthe Kollwitz was a friend and worked with Smedley translating and illustrating pamphlets on birth control. In 1928-29 Germany's most influential newspaper, the *Frankfurter Zeitung*, for which figures like Berthold Brecht and Walter Benjamin wrote, serialized *Daughter of Earth* on its front page. By then, Smedley was in China, sending reports back to the *Zeitung*.

Smedley's psychological state when she arrived in China in early 1929 appears to have been precarious. She was described at the time as mercurial, alternating between near-suicidal and paranoid moods, and moments of great compassion, mimicry, and humor. Quickly she became involved in the social and political movements of China, perhaps even more intensely than she had with India because now she saw and could directly identify with the women and poor of China. In *Yo Banfa*! Rewi Alley captures the quality of Smedley's involvement after a year in China:

> ... She had asked to be shown some factories and we had just been around some of the shocking sweatshops which were all too common in the "model settlement" of Shanghai.
>
> I can still see her great eyes look at me intently over the table as I told her of some of the suffering, some of the tragedy, some of the denial of life I moved amongst in industrial Shanghai.
>
> With a short, bitter laugh, she in her turn told me of her first vivid impression of Shanghai, how she had seen a group of workers hauling goods from a wharf on a hand cart straining under the ropes in the "tiger heat" of Shanghai summer. How there came a tall bearded Indian policeman and beat them over their bare, sweating backs to clear them out of the way of a shiny black limousine in which an arrogant foreign official sat. How she felt that it was she herself who was being beaten by that policeman, the shame she felt at seeing one of the oppressed being so treated by another of the oppressed, and how she had said to herself, "This must be a place where much can be done by anyone with guts." [6]

Alley went on to tell her how he had finally been persuaded of the impossibility of reform under the old system; it had come about when a group of men who had been organizing silk filature workers were "crudely executed at Wusih as Communist." Alley said, "It suddenly became very clear to me, that the only way was basic change. Agnes leaned forward and gripped my wrist. 'Then let's get along with the changing of it,' she said firmly."[7]

Out of such observations Smedley wrote a series of powerful reports for the *Zeitung* and for American magazines, many of which were collected in her first China book, *Chinese Destinies* (1933), some of which are reprinted in this volume. These early pieces make clear Smedley's power as a writer, and also the intensity which drew her more and more into activism. In 1931 she founded with Harold Isaacs the radical Shanghai periodical, *China Forum*, and in spring, 1932, she and Isaacs compiled a book, *Five Years of Kuomintang Reaction*, which was a bitter indictment of Chiang's government. By 1932 Smedley was subject to close surveillance and regular harassment by Kuomintang and foreign police in Shanghai. In 1932, along with Madame Sun Yat-sen and members of Academia Sinica, Smedley helped to form the League of Civil Rights in order to publicize to the outside world the absence of civil liberties under Chiang. [8] She worked closely with Madame Sun on this and other projects, although they eventually drifted apart because of personality conflicts. She tried unsuccessfully to establish a birth control clinic in Shanghai, as she had in Berlin, and she gathered material for her pioneering work on Mao and Chu Teh's Kiangsi Soviet, *China's Red Army Marches* (1934). This book was based on first-hand accounts by Communists like Red Army Commander Chou Chien-ping, who for a time had recuperated in her Shanghai apartment.

Smedley herself became seriously ill in 1933 and went to the Soviet Union to recuperate and to write *China's Red Army Marches*. After spending most of 1934 in the United States visiting family and endeavoring to find employment with United States newspapers and periodicals, she returned to China. By December, 1936, she was in the northwestern city of Sian, reporting on the famous "Incident" in which Chiang Kai-shek was kidnapped by Marshal Chang Hsueh-liang and forced to agree to ally with the Communists and go to war against Japanese imperialism. Shortly thereafter she moved to Yenan, the Communist capital, and is credited with prodding the international correspondents in China to come there to see the "red bandits" for themselves. During the war with Japan, her powerful writing and her personal commitment to relieving the wounded helped in obtaining medical supplies from abroad. Her letters to America, sent with Mao's, brought Norman Bethune and other Western doctors to China, and her personal appeal, along with Chu Teh's, to Nehru, brought five doctors and medical supplies from India. She also worked to establish the Chinese Red Cross.

Smedley had a wide range of Chinese friends including economist Ch'en Han-sheng, major writers like Lu Hsun, Mao Tun, and Ting Ling; Shanghai political figures like Madame Sun Yat-sen; and Communist leaders like Chu Teh and Chou En-lai. Among Westerners in China Smedley was well known and well liked. Her friendships were extremely varied: radicals like Anna Louise Strong, Harold Isaacs, and Frank Glass; journalists like Edgar Snow, Nym Wales, Jack Belden, Randall Gould, and Freda Utley; the British ambassador, Sir Archibald Clark-Kerr; an Episcopal Bishop, Logan Roots; Hilda Selwyne-Clarke, wife of Hong Kong's medical director; YWCA worker, Maud Russell; and the leading United States military figure in China, General Vinegar Joe Stillwell and his marine military attaché, Evans Carlson. Clearly her acquaintances spanned the political spectrum. Smedley did not hesitate to write a chapter for a book edited by Madame Chiang Kai-shek (*China Shall Rise Again*) when she saw that it would be advantageous to aiding the Chinese wounded. But her

sympathies were entirely committed to the revolutionary cause led by the Chinese Communist Party, and
especially to people like Red Army Commander Chu
Teh, whose biography she was later to write. She was
well acquainted on the Left; she had obtained her job
on the *Frankfurter Zeitung* through Julian Gumpertz,
then a member of the German Communist Party. Her
early books on China were published in the United
States by the Vanguard Press, and *China's Red Army
Marches* was also published by the Co-operative Publishing Society of Foreign Workers in the USSR as *Red
Flood Over China*. On the other hand, she remained
unwilling to have her work censored by Western Communist party people in China and she refused, during
the late 1930s, to follow the party line of attacking only
the Japanese imperialists and not Chiang Kai-shek. Some
party activists found her individualistic and difficult;
Smedley insisted she would be her own person.

In terms of her writing in the 1930s, perhaps the
most important influence upon Smedley was Lu Hsun,
the father of modern Chinese literature. She helped to
translate his work; he translated hers. Lu Hsun's vernac-
ular style and social realism reinforced Smedley's approach to writing. In 1934-35 Smedley lived with Lu
Hsun and his wife, Hsu Kuang-p'ing, for almost a year
and in 1936 they collaborated as editors of a book on
Käthe Kollwitz. [9] Smedley was also close to Ting Ling,
the well-known novelist and activist for women's causes,
with whom Smedley corresponded until her death. It
was with the help of feminists like Ting Ling that
Smedley could portray so perceptively the condition of
Chinese women in the 1920s and 1930s.

The oppression of women in traditional China is legendary. [10] In Smedley's stories we see it symbolized most
often in the brutal practice of footbinding, the reduc-
tion of the adult foot to an elegant "Golden Lily," three

inches from heel to toe. With some regional and class variation, footbinding had been the scourge of Chinese women since the tenth century. Economically and socially, women lived as family slaves, though here again the form varied from class to class and region to region. Besides housework, childbearing, and child rearing, lower-class women in southern and central China worked productively in the fields, and in both North and South, women were the backbone of a well-developed cottage textile industry. Of course, such work was done under the direction of men. Often, as Smedley suggests, lower-class women were bought or sold as *mei-tsai*—household slaves. Upper-class women did not work, but neither did they own or inherit property. They could enjoy a life of luxury and pleasure as well as command over household management, but they remained playthings and/or tools of men, be they fathers, husbands, or sons. Marriage institutionalized the subordination of upper- and lower-class women to men. To begin with, all marriages were forced, with a bride leaving her home (the wealthier with a dowry) to live and work in the home of a stranger, her husband. Only within marriage, as a breeder of males, could a woman rise in status. Otherwise, as the old proverb went, "A woman married is like a pony bought—to be ridden or whipped at the master's pleasure." Infanticide of baby girls was common among the lower classes. Traditionally, the only escape for women was suicide, prostitution, or a Buddhist nunnery.

The revolutionary process in China, for women and men, began at least as early as the mid-nineteenth century, when the traditional mandarinate and the Ch'ing dynasty were shaken to their roots by a massive peasant revolt known as the Taiping revolution (1851-64). During this revolution, footbinding was outlawed. Among the combattants were all-women divisions led by Taiping women. Women shared work and property equally with men. And women competed in the Taiping civil service examination system for places in the new Taiping bureaucracy. Eventually, overcome by superior firepower borrowed from the West, the Taipings were suppressed, but the seeds of revolution among the peasantry had been sown.

Simultaneous with the unsuccessful Taiping revolution came the onslaught of Western imperialism. Through gun-boat diplomacy and a series of wars (beginning with the Opium War of 1839-42), China was reduced to semi-colonial status by the end of the nineteenth century. It was this foreign threat, not the domestic problem of peasant unrest, that prompted upper-class Chinese to seek more drastic means to return themselves and China to the wealth and power of earlier days. By the turn of the century, reformers were moving beyond a simple borrowing of Western weaponry and technology toward an acceptance of Western social, political, and economic models for modernization. With this came an interest in women's rights. Prominent male reformers like K'ang Yu-wei and Liang Ch'i-ch'ao attacked footbinding and supported formal education for women. Footbinding was denounced as uncivilized and a symbol of China's backwardness in Western eyes; education for women was necessary if China was to become a strong modern nation state. China needed a larger and more sophisticated work force as well as educated mothers for upper-class sons.

What follows in the twentieth century, as Smedley documents in the stories in this volume, is a painful dialectic of revolutionary breakthrough countered by reactionary backlash and bloodbaths. In this way the revolution progressed, albeit slowly and tortuously, with women playing an increasingly important part. The first women revolutionaries appeared at the turn of the century. They were from the privileged classes, graduates of new educational institutions for women in China and abroad, particularly in Japan. Though influenced by Western feminist models, their feminism was distinctly different in that it was intimately tied to the new nationalism of the period. These early radical women founded a consciously feminist press in which they advocated women's rights to own property, to a free choice in marriage, to education, and to the vote. Their chief argument, however, was nationalist: China needed strong, independent women to make China strong. [11] They gave most of their time and effort to working as equals with men in the revolutionary movement led by Sun Yat-sen which aimed at the overthrow of the reigning Ch'ing dynasty and the establishment of a modern nation state governed by parliamentary means. One of the best known of these women was editor and activist Ch'iu Chin, who was executed in 1907 for leading an uprising against the Ch'ing dynasty. Women's divisions fought in the Republican revolution when it finally came in 1911-12. And with the establishment of a Republic, suffragists immediately demanded the vote, smashing windows and breaking up the National Deliberative Assembly in Peking when it was denied to them.

By 1913 the Republican revolution had fallen under the dictatorship of strong man Yuan Shih-k'ai. Revolutionaries were being killed and driven underground again. But still, intellectually if not politically, China was awash with new ideas. A sort of cultural revolution was taking place, which culminated on May 4, 1919, in a series of student demonstrations and merchant boycotts in major cities, against the selling out of Chinese sovereignty by the Western powers to Japan in the Treaty of Versailles ending World War I. Women and women's topics were in the forefront of the May Fourth Movement, helping to radicalize a new generation of women revolutionaries like Chang Siao-hung in Smedley's story "The Dedicated." The traditional family system was a major target of attack. Women demanded the right to a free marriage, to own property, to vote, to hold office, and to be educated. Ibsen's plays, especially *The Doll's House*, were being translated and performed. Footbinding was beginning to die out and women's organizations were being established in most cities and in some rural communities. And in 1919 Mao Tse-tung published his first important political essay. The subject was women, forced marriage, and suicide.

By the 1920s, politics, influenced by the May Fourth Movement, took a more progressive and nationalistic direction. In 1923-24 Sun Yat-sen reorganized his followers into the Kuomintang or Nationalist party along Soviet Bolshevik lines. He also formed an alliance with the then tiny Chinese Communist Party (established in 1921). Efforts were made to organize and politicize workers and peasants, particularly the former. In large treaty port cities like Shanghai and Canton, a trade union movement emerged in which women were important. In "Silk Workers," Smedley reports on the independence and militance of a group of Cantonese working women. Twenty thousand sister silk workers in Shanghai struck successfully in 1923 for a ten-hour day and a wage of five cents a day. Often the women leading such strikes were Communists and anarchists from upper-class backgrounds, like Hsiang Ching-yu and Ting Ling. Smedley's Chang Siao-hung in "The Dedicated" describes vividly the participation of women in major confrontations with Western imperialism, as on May 30, 1925, when British police in Shanghai opened fire on a large crowd of strikers and student demonstrators. The culmination of this Revolution, as Smedley calls it, was the successful northern expedition from 1925 to 1927 of combined Nationalist and Communist forces against the warlords of southern and central China.

The liberation of Shanghai by a workers' uprising in March, 1927, was a time of great exhilaration and hope—all to be blasted suddenly in the White Terror unleashed by the commander of the northern expeditionary forces, Chiang Kai-shek. In April, 1927, without warning, Chiang ordered all Communists rounded up and executed. Thousands died, including much of the party leadership, with the rest being driven underground. In desperation, surviving Communists attempted uprisings in a number of cities, all of which failed, bringing even greater decimation to their ranks. Women with closely-cropped hair and unbound feet, symbols of the new Chinese woman, were now hunted down as targets for persecution by the White Terror or Reaction. Smedley depicts the scene accurately in stories like "The Living Dead," "The Martyr's Widow," "The Dedicated," and "Shan-fei, Communist." In Canton on one occasion two to three hundred women were executed for having closely-cropped hair. Over one thousand women leaders were killed in the White Terror. [12] The blow to the revolution and to the women's movement was enormous, forcing major changes in direction in both.

After 1927 life seemed to go out of the major cities. Reaction set in; politically conscious youth who remained were demoralized and beaten, like Chi-yueh in "The Living Dead," or lost in a haze of pathetic adulation of Western and Japanese models, like Kwei Chu and Hsu Mei-ling and her husband. Thereafter, the battle was fought in the countryside, where an alliance formed between the men and women peasant masses and the battle-hardened leadership from the cities.

From the Taiping revolution of the mid-nineteenth century into the twentieth century, peasant revolts continued to break out. However the later rebels never reached the advanced position in regard to women or the level of organizational coherence of the Taiping revolutionaries. Not until the 1930s and the formation of Communist-led Soviets, particularly Mao and Chu

Teh's famous Kiangsi Soviet (1928-34), did large num-
bers of peasant women begin to stand up, take charge of
their lives, and fight—with their men and against them.
Important was the context of war, first civil war
between Communists and Chiang Kai-shek's Kuomintang and then, after 1936 and the Sian Incident, a
united front of these former enemies in a general
struggle for national liberation against Japanese imperialists. War accelerated economic depression, bringing
many families near or to starvation. Under pressure of
war and revolution, traditional family structures as well
as feudal bonds between landlord and tenant weakened.
In "Youth and Women's Committees," Smedley reports
how the women of the Lihwang, Anhui, area in central
China "unbound their feet, cut their hair short, studied,
and took part in public life" when the area was under
Communist control as a Soviet during the late 1920s
and early 1930s. After the Kuomintang, White forces
retook the area in the mid-1930s and reimposed reactionary rule. Women with short hair were suspect and
forced marriage was vigorously reinstated. When
Smedley visited the area in 1939, after the united front
was established, women were back in public life, holding
pivotal positions in the area's guerilla anti-Japanese
associations and struggling with their men over the
marriage issue. Lihwang, Anhui, was typical of other
guerilla areas where peasant women's potential for
egalitarian struggle, manifested earlier in the Taiping
revolution, began to resurface. All over China it was the
united front against Japan which gave the Communists
and the women's movement entrée into rural communities.

Better than any journalistic account, academic study,
or contemporary Chinese source we know of, the
portraits of Chinese women in this book document the
awakening of women, especially those from the lower
classes. In these pieces, one meets mining women,

textile workers, and peasant women like Mother Tsai, all of whom are breaking out of traditional molds and fighting for liberation. One finds radically different levels of consciousness. There were the hopelessly lost, like Hsu Mei-ling. There were the women so miserably poor that they could only strike out blindly at society, like the old woman screaming curses upon the men who laughed as she lay in the streets of Mukden. And there were radical leaders from urban upper-class backgrounds, like Chang Siao-hung in "The Dedicated" or the Communist, Shan-fei. Smedley's writing reflects the real diversity in the lives and consciousness of women in China during the 1920s and 1930s.

The stories and portraits in this volume illustrate Smedley's insistence—made clear in *Daughter of Earth* as well—upon economic self-determination for all women as the key to their independence. Economic independence would, moreover, develop in the context of the liberation of *all* oppressed people. In these respects her views were similar to those being argued during the 1930s by the Communist Chinese Women's Association. The portraits further display Smedley's admiration for strong, aggressive women, not bound even by passing obeisance to traditional proprieties. To some extent, it may be that her own indifference to such proprieties generated tensions with her Chinese comrades. One can well imagine that she startled the austere Communists when, arriving in Yenan, she threw her arms around Mao, Chou, Chu Teh, and others and gave them "big kisses." It is possible, too, that her enthusiasms—teaching the Communist leaders to square dance, for example—were mistaken for an excess of sexual liberation. At one point she apparently did generate considerable hostility by announcing that all the wives who had survived the Long March with their husbands should be divorced because they were feudal-minded. These vet-

eran women revolutionaries, who earlier had participated in experiments with the marriage law and family
relationships in a rural context, were convinced that
women would be victimized in a structureless situation
at this stage in the revolution. [13] Smedley and the
Chinese women with whom she sided on this issue had
just come from the city and had little experience in the
countryside. Mao's wife at the time, Ho Tzu-chen, once
even went so far as to threaten to kill Smedley. It is
certainly true that both Smedley and the Chinese
women envisaged relationships of sexual equality, especially among revolutionaries. Where they differed was
whether, or perhaps how, that equality should be
institutionalized. Either from outspoken views on such
subjects as sex and marriage or from other tensions
generated in her relationships with the men and women
in Yenan, Smedley was eventually asked to leave,
according to Helen Foster Snow, who was there at the
time.

Marching from Yenan in September, 1937, Smedley
wore her usual outfit, a white blouse and baggy pants.
Then, just before entering Sian, she donned a Red Army
uniform, knowing full well it would cause a sensation.
Critics later used pictures of Smedley in this uniform as
evidence of her simplistic identification with the Chinese Communist cause. Unfortunately, they missed the
point: the Red Army uniform, not her usual garb, was
put on in order to stir up publicity and bring attention
to a cause. Smedley realized the distance that separated
her from the Chinese and knew that she could never
fully identify with them, even given her own working-
class background. This theme runs through most of her
books. As she wrote in *China Fights Back*:

Tonight as these hungry men sang, and then as they
marched away to their beds of straw or cornstocks
spread on mud floors, their singing had more meaning

to me than ever before. Their voices were like a string orchestra in the night. I, who have food this day, realized that I can never know fully the meaning, the essence of the Chinese struggle for liberation, which lies embedded in the hearts of these workers and peasants. I am still an onlooker and my position is privileged. I will always have food though these men hunger. I will have clothing and a warm bed though they freeze. They will fight and many of them will die on frozen battlefields. I will be an onlooker. I watched them blend with the darkness of the street; they still sang. And I hungered for the spark of vision that would enable me to see into their minds and hearts and picture their convictions about the great struggle for which they give more than their lives. [14]

Smedley spent 1938 living in Hankow, waiting for the expected Japanese attack. Her wholehearted dedication to the causes she believed in brought her respect and admiration from such diverse people as Communist representative Chou En-lai, Kuomintang Finance Minister T.V. Soong, British ambassador Sir Archibald Clark-Kerr, anti-Communist journalist Freda Utley, American consul-general John Davies, *New York Times* reporter Tilman Durdin, pro-Communist war correspondent Jack Belden, and—her closest friend—United States Marine officer Evans Carlson. She worked officially with Dr. Robert K.S. Lim on publicity for the Chinese Red Cross and was a special correspondent for the *Manchester Guardian*. During this period Smedley was particularly effective in bringing together people with very different political concerns and became more obviously self-confident, humorous, and warm.

After the fall of Hankow in October, 1938, Smedley joined the Communist-led New Fourth Army. Her days with the army are vividly described in *Battle Hymn of China* (Knopf, 1943), generally considered to be one of the best books of war reporting to come out of World War II. In summary, she shared the incredible hardships of war and helped to set up Red Cross stations and to minister first aid to the wounded. She was also a very effective speaker at mass rallies. In 1950 Liu Liang-mou recalled her rising with great difficulty because of ill health to speak to a large crowd in Changsha. Once on her feet, she was transformed into a ferocious and passionate speaker, her rhetoric profoundly stirring the crowd. [15]

Although her work with the New Fourth Army was fulfilling in terms of serving a cause, a certain sense of personal isolation is revealed in the following letter, written to Freda Utley in June, 1939, while Smedley was with the guerillas.

Dearest Freda,

The last days of Hankow still remain in my mind as rare, unusual days from the psychological and human viewpoint. I still think of Shaw's "Heartbreak House" when I recall them. As you remarked at the time, no person on earth is more charming than the American journalist abroad, particularly the cultured, serious-minded ones. But I wonder what it would be like were I to meet those same men on the streets of Chicago. Gone the Magic! The only ones who have maintained some contact with me were Evans and Frank. Evans wrote me a short note from Shanghai and sent it here by Belden who came here for a week. Then Evans remembered to send me a copy of one of his articles in *Amerasia*. And, as Frank Dorn [United States Naval officer] returned to America, he wrote me a long, human letter from the ship. But then a ship is much like Hankow—an island on which one is thrown back upon oneself. I suppose he has forgotten me by this time. Once Durdin asked someone in Chungking where I am—so he remembers I am somewhere in the land of the living.

I sort of pine for the magic of Hankow. It was the bright spot in one decade of my life. There I met foreign men, some of them rotters, but most of them with the charm that belongs to many men of the Western world. They themselves do not know how very different they are from the Chinese. Though I have never liked to be treated as bourgeois women are treated, still the foreign men from England, America, and perhaps France, have a deep and unconscious attitude of respect for women; a little feeling of protection for women; of helping a woman; and a kind of gentleness toward her. Often his kindness blended a bit with tenderness or a breath of romance. It is difficult to explain, because it is there as an atmosphere. In the Chinese man this is totally lacking in all respects. There is not even friendship and comradeship between man and woman in China. The foreign word "romance" has been taken into the Chinese language and means promiscuous sexual relations. And "love" means sexual intercourse in its general use in China. For a Chinese man to even touch a woman's arm or hand means something sexual and arouses shock.

So, for ten years I lived in this desert, and because of this, I found a magical place. Since then I have thought much of this. Shall I return to the western world, or shall I remain here? I fear I must remain in China. Hankow was a rare exception, and I believe all of us felt the same about it. I wish to retain it as a precious memory. I think often of the play in which many persons of different classes are on a foundering ship in mid-ocean. Class distinctions fall away as they face death together, drawn closer by humanity. But when the storm passes and the ship is saved, the old cold and cruel class distinctions returned. I believe that to be Hankow.

Love,
Agnes [16]

Agnes Smedley's closest emotional tie during this period was with a ten-year-old boy orderly, Shen Kuo-hwa, whom she wanted to adopt as her Chinese son. Her story of their relationship (reprinted in this volume) was so admired by Hemingway that he included it in a book he edited during World War II called *Men at War*.

Increased danger from the Japanese in 1940 and ill health caused Smedley to leave her beloved New Fourth Army. To its leaders, a continuation of her influential writing was top priority. She went to Chungking, then the Nationalist capital, but because her health was fragile she was ordered to Hong Kong by Dr. Lim. In September, 1940, she made her way to Kweilin, Kwang-si, and then flew over Japanese lines to Hong Kong. For a while she recuperated there with her friend Hilda Selwyne-Clarke. Then, with the fall of Hong Kong imminent, she borrowed money from Evans Carlson to return to her estranged family in San Diego.

During the 1940s Smedley produced her most important work. She continued to write book reviews for several journals including the *New Republic*, but her main tasks, outside of lecturing on and talking about China, were to complete *Battle Hymn of China* (which was translated almost immediately into Chinese) and to start the Chu Teh biography. After publication and deserved critical praise for *Battle Hymn* in 1943-44, Smedley achieved relative peace in her personal life. Her friendships with leading China war correspondents Edgar Snow and Jack Belden deepened; her book, lectures, radio programs, and radio debates with such persons as ex-missionary and Congressman Walter Judd proved her mastery over herself and her material. She spent the mid-1940s at the writers' colony, Yaddo, in upstate New York. There she acquired many new and valued friends, including Katherine Ann Porter, Carson McCullers, and Toni and George Willison. Her interest in drama continued. Besides going to the theater whenever possible, she worked on a play about the liberation of Chinese women by the Chinese Communist Party. She also loved to root around in gardens in these years. Her interest was in "a good tomato," not beautiful flowers.

Smedley's life of relative peace and productivity ended abrutly on February 10, 1949, when the United States Army released a report, produced by General MacArthur's staff, on the Sorge spy ring which accused her of having been a Soviet spy since the early 1930s. Smedley immediately went to court, forcing the army to recant publicly. But in a political atmosphere charged with anti-communism, allegations continued that Smedley was a Communist or subversive of some sort. [17] It became impossible for her to find enough work to support herself.

When the news of Communist victory in China came in October, 1949, Smedley was ecstatic. She was also fed up with America; so, despite her poor health, she decided to return to China. Smedley went to London, intending to wait there for a visa. On May 4, 1950, she underwent surgery in an Oxford hospital to have two-thirds of her stomach removed because of ulcers. On May 6, Agnes Smedley died. A few days later in a Quaker meeting house in New York, a simple, plain-speaking memorial service was held, led by Edgar Snow and attended by two hundred friends.

There was little public mourning over Agnes Smedley's death anywhere except in China. There, lead articles in Chinese newspapers by Ting Ling, Mao Tun, and other friends mourned her death. These were republished in a commemorative volume together with selected translations of her work. The Chinese expressed outrage, bitterly accusing the United States government of murder for hounding Smedley into destitution and a fatal illness because she supported the Chinese people. [18] In 1960 Premier Chou En-lai opened his first interview with Edgar Snow in over twenty years with a salute to the memory of Agnes Smedley and Franklin D. Roosevelt. [19] Today Smedley remains a heroine in Chinese eyes and is buried in honor outside Peking. But in the United States her name continued for many years to be subject to insult and ridicule. [20] In 1956 when one of her most important works, *The Great Road: The Life and Times of Chu Teh*, was published by Monthly Review Press, it was hardly noticed. By the 1960s, Agnes Smedley was all but forgotten. [21]

It has taken the resurgence of a new women's movement, of a new Left, and of a new concern for China to reawaken interest in Smedley as a writer and a person. She would have liked it that way. For as the first section of *Battle Hymn of China* illustrates, she did not separate her own life history from the chronicle of the Chinese revolution. Rather, in that book and elsewhere, she set her own life, as she set her own writing, in the context of a struggle for fundamental social change and for liberation from every form of bondage.

The stories and sketches which follow are selected from a variety of Smedley's works and put more or less in chronological order. Most are drawn from books; some first appeared as newspaper or magazine reports. In addition to the material in this volume, Smedley wrote other pieces on women, such as the sketches of prisoners in "Cell Mates," articles on birth control, and studies of Indian women. While she remained deeply interested in the lives of women, she never thought to collect in one volume all she had written about them. There was no active women's movement asking for such a collection and, moreover, she saw the struggles of women in the context of the larger social and political movements of her day.

This volume documents not only the pain and sacrifice that were part of the struggle for the liberation of women in China; it also shows that in China the women's and revolutionary movements came to be necessarily intermeshed and dependent upon one another for success. Smedley's stories may speak to us more vividly today since the women's movement in the West is searching for direction, learning the difficulties of overcoming setbacks, and discovering its connections with larger political movements. Of course, no two historical situations are identical, but perhaps, as Smedley thought, Western women can learn from the Chinese experience.

Notes

1. *The Call Magazine*, 15 February 1920; 22 February 1920; 29 February 1920; 14 March 1920.

2. Joan Jensen, "Outcasts in a Savage Land: The Politics of East Indian Immigration, 1900-17" (unpublished manuscript) and Alan Raucher, "American Anti-Imperialists and the Pro-India Movement, 1900-1932," *Pacific Historical Review* 43 (February 1974): 83-110.

3. Emma Goldman, *Living My Life* (New York: Alfred A. Knopf, 1931), p. 905.

4. M.N. Roy, *M.N. Roy's Memoirs* (Bombay and New York: Allied Publishers, 1964), p. 488.

5. "Die Indische Frau von gestern und Heute," *Frau, Monatschrift für das Besamte Frauenieben Unserer Zeit* 32 (1924): 239-44, 279-83; "Indiens als Entscheidener Faktor der Weltpolitik," *Zeitschrift fur Geopolitik* 2, no. 6 (June 1925): 385-403; "Der Kommende Krieg gegen Asien," *International* (Arbeiter-Association) 2, no. 64 (1925): 22-26; "Die Frau in Indien," *Neue Zürcher Zeitung*, 12 August 1925, Blatt 4;

"Freiwilliger Opfertod bei den Hindus," *Neue Zürcher Zeitung*, 24 December 1925; "Indiens Nationale Füherin," *Deutche Allgemeine Zeitung*, 31 December 1925; "Die Inderin von Heute," *Neue Generation: Zeitschrift fur Mutterschietz und Sexual Reform*, (21 J. [20 J. fehlt nock] 1925): 95-100; "Indien Fuhrerin (Sarojini Naidu)," *Frau in Staat: Eine Monatschrift* 8, No. 4, (1926): 52; "Indien Dichterin, *Beliner Tageblatt*, 4 September 1926; "Die Neger Renaissance," *Der Philologe*, 3. folger, No. 6, 15 March 1928, p. 1 (this was a student publication at the University of Berlin). Articles in English which Smedley published during her German period included: "Jodh Singh," *The Nation*, 22 March 1922, pp. 341-42; "Starving Germany," *The Nation*, 28 November 1923, pp. 601-2; "Akali Movement: An Heroic Epic," *The Nation*, 2 July 1924, pp. 15-17; "Germany's Red Front," *The Nation*, 1 August 1928, pp. 116-17; "Writing Since the War," *Survey*, 1 February 1929, p. 596, co-authored with Julian Gumpertz.

6. Rewi Alley, *Yo Banfa!* (Peking: New World Press, 1952), pp.15-16.

7. *Ibid.*, p.16.

8. The Academia Sinica was the state supported national academy of China's intellectual elite. Prominent intellectuals from Academia Sinica who participated with Smedley in the League of Civil Rights included writer Lu Shun and scholar-educators Ts'ai Yuan-pei and Hu Shih.

9. This is what Lu Hsun's wife, Hsu Kuang-p'ing, told Ayako Ishigaki in 1955. Ayako Ishigaki, *Kaiso no Sumedore* (Remembering [Agnes] Smedley) (Tokyo: Misuzu Shobō, 1967), p. 64.

10. The best single reference and bibliography on Chinese women is Marilyn Young, ed., *Women in China*, Michigan Papers in Chinese Studies, no. 15 (Ann Arbor: Center for Chinese Studies, 1973). Another important recent work is Margery Wolf and Roxanne Witke, eds., *Women in Chinese Society* (Stanford: Stanford University .Press, 1975). A short, broad survey which is readily available is Sheila Rowbotham's chapter, "When the Sand-Grouse Flies to Heaven" in her *Women, Resistance, and Revolution* (New York: Vintage, 1974).

11. Charlotte L. Beahan, "Feminism and Nationalism in the Chinese Women's Press, 1902-1911," *Modern China* 1, no. 4 (October 1975): 379-416.

12. Helen F. Snow (Nym Wales), *Women in Modern China* (Hague and Paris: Mouten, 1967), p. 242 and *Inside Red China* (New York: Doubleday, Doran & Co., 1939), p. 170.

13. On earlier experiments see Chi-hsi Hu, "The Sexual Revolution in the Kiangsi Soviet," *China Quarterly* 59 (July-September 1974): 477-490.

14. *China Fights Back* (New York: The Vanguard Press, 1938), p.123.

15. *Shih-mo-t'e-lai—Chung-kuo jen-min chih yu* ([Agnes] Smedley—Friend of the Chinese People) (Peking: Hsin-hua Shu-tien, 1950), pp.40-41.

16. Freda Utley, *Odyssey of a Liberal* (Washington, D.C.: Washington National Press, 1970), pp.206-07.

17. The most detailed, explicit attacks on Smedley were made by Major General Charles A. Willoughby in his book, *Shanghai Conspiracy: The Sorge Spy Ring* (New York: E.P. Dutton & Co., 1952). Chalmers Johnson vindicates Smedley of such charges in his more objective, scholarly work, *An Instance of Treason: Ozaki Hotsumi and the Sorge Spy Ring* (Stanford: Stanford University Press, 1964).

18. *Shih-mo-t'e-lai—Chung-kuo jen-min chih yu* (full citation in note 15). See also major articles in English commemorating the anniversary of her death, in *People's China*, 16 May 1951, pp.13-14 and 16 May 1953, p.36. *People's China* was the predecessor of *Peking Review*.

19. Edgar Snow, *The Other Side of the River* (New York: Random House, 1961), p.77.

20. Typical are the snide comments about Smedley in Kenneth E. Shewmaker, *Americans and Chinese Communists, 1927-45: A Persuading Encounter* (Ithaca: Cornell University Press, 1971).

21. The exception was Japan. There a translation of her Chu Teh biography sold well and in 1967 Ayako Ishigaki, a good friend of Smedley's from the 1940s, published the first and to date the only biography—*Kaiso no Sumedore* (cited in note 9).

THE SONG OF SUFFER- ING

One night, in a little Chinese inn in the interior, a Chinese girl from Kwangtung lay on a huge carved Chinese bed and related stories of her child life. Her own name was taken from an ancient Chinese folk ballad, and this song she had known from her earliest dawn of consciousness. She sang it, her two frail white hands folded together beneath her head.

As in most folk ballads the song was simple, relating a story in many stanzas. In such folk music the wierdness of classical Chinese music vanishes, and here was a song that the most Westernized of persons could understand. The song was more than just a ballad; it was folk memory; and it was a symbol that can and does mean many things today in China. But, literally, it is the song

Chinese Destinies: Sketches of Present-Day China (New York: The Vanguard Press, 1933), pp. 313-15.

of a sorrowing wife whose husband was killed building Chang Ch'eng, or the Great Wall, two hundred years before the beginning of the Christian Era. The song begins:

The first month is new Spring.
Red lanterns hang on every building.
Other husbands return homeward,
Only my husband is building Chang Ch'eng.

The second month, pairs of swallows
Fly to the southern wall.
They sleep on columns under the roof,
But my home is empty and austere.

The song continues thus for twelve stanzas. In the third month there are pink peach blossoms and green willows, and the families burn incense in their ancestral tombs. The fourth month is the month of roses and of mulberry leaves to feed the silk worms. The fifth month tells of yellow plums, when every family is cultivating its land and only the land of the family Wan lies idle. The lotus blossoms in the sixth month, and in the seventh month the honeysuckle flourishes luxuriantly and the women sew before the windows. In the eighth month the yellow cassia blossoms, and the messenger pigeons return home with letters from absent ones. But no letter comes for the lonely wife whose husband has died a thousand *li* away. In the ninth month the pilgrims go on journeys, and there are fine wine and gorgeous chrysanthemums. In the tenth month the *fulung* tree rises above the wall and "peasants harvest their rice to pay their taxes." With the snowfall in the eleventh month the hoarfrost glistens on every dried grass blade. And in the twelfth month the yellow wax flowers blossom, and there are preparations for new year's rejoicing. But the lonely wife whose husband has been killed building Chang Ch'eng weeps at home until her sorrow reaches the very heaven and even the Great Wall listens and crumbles.

This ancient song was sung in a gentle, sweet voice. The song seems to be sung in every nook and corner of China.

One may ask why, and there are many Chinese who will tell you: it is because the building of Chang Ch'eng, or the Great Wall, touched practically every family in China at that time. Two thousand and five hundred miles of great and magnificent walls were built within twenty years and, like the Pyramids of Egypt or the Hanging Gardens of Babylon, they were built by slave labor.

It is said that three out of every ten men in the Chinese Empire were called upon to help build the Great Wall, and that they were driven like beasts under the lash of cruel taskmasters. When they fell, exhausted, injured, or dying, their bodies were buried in the earthwork of the wall itself. And the tale of its building has come down the centuries, its memories lingering in this folk song, as in many others.

This one song, so universally known and sung in China, has come to be a symbol not so much of suffering at the building of the Great Wall, as of suffering in general. Today in the streets of Shanghai you can hear the coolies sing it, but in transformed version. It is now a revolutionary song, a song retaining part of the original words, as also the entire music of the original. But the rest of it is a story of the revolution which the people built but which was then betrayed by the Kuomintang.

Now, says the song, the bitter sorrow of the people reaches the very heavens until the Great Wall itself listens and crumbles. The words are partly lyrical, partly militant. But the music remains wistful, burdened with a melancholy common to almost all folk songs.

THE DEDI-CATED

Across the great historical stage on which the Chinese revolution is being played, appears and reappears the figure of a woman.

At first the figure looks delicate and the hands as frail as those of a child; but when one sees more clearly, the slender body, of a little more than ordinary height, looks tough and wiry and the hands but thin from constant labor. The hair, smooth and black as a soft summer's night, is sometimes cropped close like a boy's, sometimes grown longer and clasped at the nape of the neck in a narrow brooch of green. At times the figure is

Chinese Destinies: Sketches of Present-Day China, pp. 68-89. The reference to eighteen Lohan is to the personal disciples of Buddha (two Chinese, sixteen Indian) whose images were often in local temples. The sense here is of the eighteen Lohan as good luck charms. Smedley wrote in greater detail in German about the *mei-tsai* or domestic slave girls of Hong Kong (see "Mui-tsai" (sic), *Frankfurter Zeitung*, September 10, 1930).

clad in the uniform of a soldier, at other times in the faded cotton trousers and jacket of a woman of the masses; and at still other times in the elegant silk gown of a lady of the ruling classes.

This slight figure, now clad in a long silk gown that falls in an unbroken line from the throat to the ankles, turns her face to us. The face belies the costume. For here is none of the expressionless, doll-like beauty, or the cold passive indifference, or any of the calculating selfishness or cruelty that characterize the faces of women of the ruling classes. Instead, the face turned toward us is lit by some fire that gives the eyes and entire countenance an expression of some living, burning conviction. It is a face of inspired intelligence. The eyes, black and shining, see everything, understand everything. In every action of the figure, in every word uttered on this vast historical stage, are expressed two forces: one, love and passion; the other, a conviction that is hard and unyielding in its purpose.

The woman may speak for herself, as do many actors on the old feudal stage of China, who often step forward to explain what rôle they are playing. It is best that the woman speak quickly, lest tragedy overtake her and silence her tongue forever. So, let her speak:

"My name is Chang Siao-hung. I was born in 1902 of a very rich and well-known family of Hong Kong. All the wealth of the large joint family of which I am a member was earned by my grandfather, who began life as the servant of a British enterpriser.

"A few years after China was defeated in the Opium Wars and was forced to admit opium to the country, pay heavy indemnities, grant concessions of land, and cede Hong Kong to the British, this Englishman offered my grandfather money and credit if he would help him exploit the new colony. This offer was accepted, and after a number of years my grandfather's share in the property was valued at ten million *taels*, including land, houses, godowns, shops, wharves, gambling houses and the opium traffic.

"Because he was from a very poor family, my grandfather had not received a feudalistic education; and since he had always been in close touch with Western capitalists, he was much influenced by capitalist ideas and methods. Socially he retained many feudal customs, and with these he united capitalist methods of exploitation that enabled him to squeeze wealth for his family out of every workingman and woman that crossed his path.

"Because of his wealth he was much honored and admired by the old people of South China, yet many disapproved of some of his new ideas, such as the education of the women of his family. Fortunately my sisters and I were permitted to receive an education, and some of the men of our family went to foreign lands to study. But such free ideas extended only to my grandfather's own family; never to the families of others or to the masses of the people. For like his British partner he poisoned the masses with opium, and he sold men and women into slavery.

"My grandmother was a very cunning and capable woman of the old school, and despite the wealth of the family she was never satisfied unless more money was pouring through her fingers into the family coffers. After my grandfather died, shortly before the overthrow of the Manchu Dynasty, my grandmother became almost supreme authority in our home. This was because my father, who as eldest son should have assumed his position as head of the family, was sunk in opium smoking and cared little for anything but personal indulgence. My own mother was the capable and ambitious daughter of a big salt merchant, and she was a perfect support for my grandmother.

"I had two sisters and four brothers, but my mother seemed to love me, the youngest child, more than any of her children. This was more than unusual, for I was a girl, and it is said that even a club-footed son is of more value than a daughter with the virtues of eighteen Lohans, while to educate a daughter is said to be like watering another man's garden.

"When I was six years old, one of the men of our large family returned from abroad and established a coeducational school in Hong Kong. He induced my mother and grandmother to permit me to lead the way for girls by attending this school. This caused a great sensation at the time, for coeducation was not permitted by either the Chinese or British.

"While my family was thus penetrated by modern ideas in some respects, it remained feudal and colonial in others; and, like other foreign and Chinese merchants in South China, it was rooted in the purest kind of mercenary commercialism. Money-making was the one aim of existence, the one thing treasured, the one god before whom all bowed in cringing respect. Money-making excused everything, explained everything, and to it everything in life was subordinated.

"One of my earliest memories was of the slave trade in which my grandmother took a part. For, as I said, she was a woman never satisfied unless money was pouring through her fingers. The slaves in whom she dealt were always girls, courteously called *mui tsai*—which literally means domestic drudge—and there are Chinese and British apologists who try to dignify their lot by calling them 'adopted daughters.'

"This phrase is one of the many whited sepulchers of China. The *mui tsai* are slaves, bought and sold for money, and their owners have the power of life and death over them; they can be resold whenever or wherever it pleases the fancy of their owners; they may be sent as workers into the factories to earn money for their owners; they may be used as prostitutes; they may be sold to rich and degenerate men as concubines. These girls are the daughters of peasants of South China provinces, peasants so poor that they cannot afford the luxury of maintaining their daughters until they can be married into other families.

"There are few homes even of moderate means in South China and Hong Kong that do not have one or more girl slaves who do all the heavy drudgery of the household. The beautiful girls are usually sold for high prices as concubines of rich men. Still others are sold as prostitutes into the sing-song houses or to the 'flower boats'—that is, the brothels—of Canton, Macao, Hong Kong, or all the cities of the South Seas. Beautiful Cantonese concubines or prostitutes are also much sought after by the rich of Shanghai and other North China cities.

"Our own home rested upon the labor of such girl slaves, for all of our servants were *mui tsai*. More still. Into our home were brought girls to be sold to the rich men of our class. My grandmother did the selling. As a tiny child I recall standing by my grandmother's side when men came to look at these girls. Sometimes it was a fat official from Canton, or a rich merchant, or the sensuous and lazy son of merchants or officials of Canton or Hong Kong. They came looking for concubines. Less often it was a man or woman seeking household slaves. When such men called in their long, flowing silk gowns, they would be served tea, and my grandmother would express concern about the health and prosperity of their honorable families.

"Then, when the purpose of their visit was finally discussed, the girls would be brought in, nicely dressed for the occasion, their faces beautifully powdered and painted. But the buyers were very cunning business men and could not be cheated, and often they would compel the girl to lift her long, broad trousers or her gown that they might see the color of the skin on her legs. Now and then a man would take a cloth, wet it, and rub the powder off a girl's face to make certain the skin was fair beneath. And there were times when he would feel her body here and there.

"When satisfied, the man would go close to the girl, grin sensuously into her face, and ask: 'Would you like to be my concubine?' The girl, her head bowed to her chest, would answer 'Yes.' And big tears would roll from her eyes, leaving long traces on her sad face. Then she would withdraw and the purchaser would bargain with my grandmother; but before paying the full price he would often insist upon proof that his commodity was a virgin. If after the first night he found she was not, he would return her and demand his money back.

"Some men have chosen to say the taking of a concubine is a 'love mating,' and that although the first wife is the conventional way of maintaining the family and providing for the worship of ancestors, the concubine system provides for the element of love. But I ask—love for whom? The concubine is a slave, bought and sold, and she can be resold if it please the fancy of her master or if he becomes poor and needs money. Or she may be presented by her influential owner to one of his subordinates. Love! This purchase of helpless poor women by rich men is what the ruling class of my country call love. But even for the men who buy these women it is nothing but physical lust.

"Do you think I speak of the dark ages, of the past, or even of a quarter of a century ago when I was a child—of customs dead and gone? No, I speak of the present. For women and girls are sold into slavery in North, South, East, and West China today; and as my country has sunk into deeper poverty and deeper subjection, so has the buying and selling of slaves sunk deeper roots. The highest officials and militarists in the various governments, whether Nanking, Canton, or Peking, have their purchased concubines, and Chiang Kai-shek, whom the foreigners so admire and support, 'put away' four 'wives' in order to marry a woman on whose connections he expected to build his personal and political fortunes.

"I was the daughter of a wealthy family, blessed with every comfort that money could buy. My mother loved me dearly, protected me, planned for my future happiness. But even as a little child I used to wonder what would have happened to me had I been born the daughter of a peasant or some other poor man, as were the girls in our kitchen and those who passed through the lady-like hands of my grandmother. Even as a little child I could never forget the tears of girls as they said 'yes' to some rich man as they were being sold, and in my childhood fantasies I thought of myself as the general of a powerful army going forth to fight and free all the slave girls.

"In my childhood I also heard of the trade in men slaves, many of whom were kidnaped, while others were shipped abroad under various guises that were supposed to satisfy the consciences of the 'sentimentalists.' One of these guises, in use down to the living present, is called contract labor. Poor peasants, workingmen, or disbanded soldiers of South China are induced by promises of high monthly wages, by tales of great riches, or even by simple offers of enough to fill their empty stomachs, to enlist by the thousands for labor on the plantations or in the mines of British, Dutch, or French colonies in southeastern Asia, which we call Nanyang, or the South Seas.

"One often hears of the wealth accumulated by Chinese 'emigrants' to Nanyang. A few, indeed, accumulate wealth. But for every such man tens of thousands die in poverty and despair, often under the lash of cruel task-masters. Some send back money to their families and it is millions in the year; but there are millions of men of my country forced to seek livelihood in the colonies of foreign imperialist countries, and if they can send back three or four dollars a month from their meager earnings it mounts into the millions. But for each man it is but a miserable pittance.

"I can bring you closer to this method of sending men to the plantations and mines of European colonies now in these modern days. In Hong Kong there is a branch of a great Dutch trading company that supplies workers for the tin mines of the Dutch East Indies, mines lying in such an unhealthy territory that men live but a short span of years there. Yet two or three times a year this Dutch Company sends Chinese labor recruiters into Kwangtung Province to relate tales of the riches awaiting men who will go to the Dutch East Indies. The labor recruiter is paid a number of dollars per head, and this he shares with the Chinese official who permits this recruiting and who gives passports to the victims.

"The recruits are shipped, in lots of a few hundred, to Hong Kong, where the Dutch Company examines them to see if their chests are broad, their arms and bodies strong enough to do the work that no men in the Dutch East Indies will do. From Hong Kong these men are packed together in transport ships in which cattle could not be transported and live, and shipped away. Arriving at a port in the Dutch East Indies, they are landed and confined in pens where legal documents in the Dutch language are placed before them to sign. Unable to read even their own language, they certainly cannot read Dutch, and knowing nothing of legal documents they are helpless before them. Nor were they ever told that they would be forced to put their fingerprints on a document that signs away their freedom as human beings for ten long years.

"For this document binds them to labor in the tin mines for ten years at a wage set by the Dutch and

under conditions that make them slaves. This document
was not laid before them in China where they would
have had a chance to choose. But now, if they refuse to
sign, they are informed that they must repay the
company for the passage and food to this strange land,
and they must leave the country at once and pay their
own passage back to China. If they still protest, there is
the boot of their new Dutch owners, and there is the
lash, freely used. In despair most of them sign because
they are bound to the wheel of poverty and ignorance;
and those who object, as do a few one-time soldiers
whom the Dutch call 'bad elements,' sign anyway,
because 'to fight is but to die, and to return is but to
mingle with the desert sands.'

"And then they are transported to the tin mines
where so many die that new shipments of men are made
twice a year. Those who try to escape are captured and
brought to trial before a court whose judges are the
managers of the mines; and as punishment there is the
lash and a prolongation of the contract of slavery.

"Today among the slave-owners in Nanyang are not
merely British, Dutch, French and Americans. There are
now Chinese millionaires. These are sons of Chinese
fathers who spent their lives in hard toil or who, by
unusual and devious means, accumulated great fortunes.
These men have now joined the class front of the white
owners of plantations and mines. Racial lines have
vanished and there has emerged only hard class lines,
drawn in the blood of the workers on whose bodies the
wealth of Nanyang rests.

". . . But I have wandered from my own personal
story. I thought this story of human slavery would
interest you; for it is one of the countless facts of
human subjection that awakened me to my duty, that
showed me the face of the ruling class.

"I was telling you that my family was a mixture of
feudal practices and of modern capitalist ideas, and that

when it combined the two methods of exploitation it pressed a great fortune out of the bodies of those that came within its power. By the accident of birth into such a family and at such a period, I was able to go to school and to enjoy many rights that girls of former periods and in other parts of China could not enjoy. When I was a child the Manchu Dynasty was overthrown and a flood of new ideas poured through my country. Men and boys cut off their cues, the symbol of subjection, and women and girls in the centers of ferment no longer bound their feet. My own feet were never bound.

"But one of the most important periods of my life began May 4, 1919, when I was sixteen years of age. One of my sisters had married a number of years before and was living in Canton where her husband was a high official. She was fortunate that her husband's family lived in Swatow and that she could have her own individual home in Canton. But she was very unhappy because her life was one endless round of bearing children. She now had seven children and each year a new one arrived, leaving her weaker and in deeper despair. Her husband spent most of his life at banquets of officials, in gambling and with sing-song girls.

"My mother had permitted me to go to Canton and live with my sister during my period of study in the middle school. It was here that I was living when the May fourth movement was begun by the students and professors of Peking National University. They held great demonstrations against the Peace Conference of Versailles when the imperialist powers posing as China's friends set their seals of approval upon Japanese occupation of Chinese territory and upon the infamous Twenty-one Demands which Japan had forced upon the old and corrupt Peking Government. This movement forced the Chinese delegates to withdraw from the Peace Conference.

"But for the youth of China, especially the intellectual youth, the May fourth movement was more than political. It came closely upon the heels of the great October Revolution in Russia, bringing with it a reappraisal of all social values; and it dealt a death-blow to feudal ideas in the intellectual young. In Canton the students were much more free and vigorous than those in British Hong Kong, and I was intoxicated by this movement. It was like a fresh, invigorating breeze through a musty and ancient dwelling.

"The leading professors and students of Peking National University were publishing the *New Youth*, a magazine that introduced the intellectual renaissance into China. One of the founders of the Chinese Communist Party was its editor. Through this magazine I came into contact with Marxian doctrine and began the serious study of the social sciences. I was at the time a member of the Kwangtung Students' Union, which was very radical, and I became one of its leaders.

"In that year we students of Canton organized schools for poor children, and from this time onward I learned not merely to pity and sympathize with the poor but to place my knowledge at their disposal, to serve them because all that I enjoyed in life came out of their bodies. And during the two following years in Canton, I spent almost all my free time out of school as a teacher in the workers' night schools. I never seemed to tire, for the workers who came to study were like the thirsty seeking water in a desert.

"This same period of my life, filled with hard work and a great purpose, was also filled with great struggles with my family. With the exception of my two sisters, both of whom were unhappily married, every member of my large family tried to force me into marriage. It was not merely my mother who pleaded with me, the tears rolling down her cheeks, but it was my brothers, my uncles, aunts, cousins, and all the variations of these relatives, until about a hundred people were bent upon the one goal of rescuing me from my 'dangerous tendencies' and binding me to a marriage with some young millionaire. Repeatedly I refused to marry, but my mother would only seek some other young millionaire whom she thought would please me more. Every visit to my Hong Kong home was filled with misery and struggle; every visit my relatives made to my sister's home in Canton, every letter that came to me, were filled with new suffering for me.

"But I refused, with firm decision, to marry, and I was determined to study, become a physician, and serve the workers and peasants of China. This struggle with my family was my first great struggle with feudalistic influences, and it was a fearful struggle that closed in upon me from every direction for a period of over two years.

"I was eighteen when my eldest sister, married to a high official in the Peking Government, secretly sent me money to escape from Canton and go to her in Peking. One day I left Canton, went to Hong Kong, boarded a ship without the knowledge of my family, and left. For many years I did not return. From Peking I wrote my mother, asking her for money to study medicine in Peking, and threatening, if she refused, never to see her again. Finally her love for me prevailed, and she bowed her sad, confused head to my wishes.

"In Peking I became a student in the famous Peking National University, and along with my preparatory studies for the profession of medicine I began the thorough and serious study of Marxism. I read many books, many short stories and articles, many translations; and I came into intimate contact with writers for such publications as *New Youth* and *Creative Society*, the latter issued by a new literary society founded by

Communist intellectuals in Shanghai. My whole student period in Peking was filled with hard work; and the more I studied of medicine, the more it became clear to me that most diseases are social and would not even exist in a free Communist society.

"I had studied in Peking for five years when the May thirtieth movement began. This movement followed upon the massacre of students and workers by the British police of Shanghai, May 30, 1925. Far more than the May fourth incident this massacre revealed to us that imperialism is the great hindrance to the advancement of China. We determined to fight it down. In the worker and student strikes, and in the anti-British boycott that swept through the country after this, I became very active. But in the following year still new forces inimical to China's progress were clearly thrown into high light, for on March eighteenth in Peking the Chinese police massacred a large number of students demonstrating against an ultimatum by the imperialists—an ultimatum before which our Chinese rulers not only crawled, but shot down those who protested.

"I was in the demonstration when the massacre began. The police raised their rifles and began to shoot into the mass meeting where thousands of students, including young children, were gathered. When the crowd began to escape from the rain of bullets, the police shot them in the backs. I stood, unable to move for some time, watching the police lift their rifles, fire into the backs of fleeing youths, laugh, and fire again. Deliberately they shot down people as if they were shooting birds, and there was something so unbelievable about it, something so inhuman, so barbarous in the way it was done, that I could not turn away.

"Then I turned and tried to go away. But I stumbled and fell, and I found I had fallen upon the body of a girl, the blood streaming in a slow, dark rivulet from her neck. Then something fell upon me heavily, and something else, pinning me to the body beneath me. Unable to stir, I heard agonizing gasps, felt the quivering and convulsions of the bodies above me, and something warm and reeking began to pour all over me, through my clothing, down over my neck and my face. From afar I heard the crack, crack, crack of rifles and the screams of men and women. I cried for help and through my mind flowed a sense of utmost futility, blended with cold horror. Then I knew no more until hurrying voices awoke me and I opened my eyes to find girl comrades in my dormitory washing the blood from me, while a doctor was feeling my body.

"In this massacre the bodies of my school comrades saved my life. The only injury I received was a bullet wound through the upper part of my arm. I had not even felt this. But this massacre showed us another enemy to the progress of China—the militarists and officials.

"In the spring of this same year I became, after six years of study in Peking, a physician. I had originally planned to go to some foreign country to continue my studies, but the revolutionary movement was very high and its army was planning to leave Canton and march against the militarists of the North. So I left Peking at once and hurried to Canton, which was the revolutionary center of China.

"Since I had left Canton the great general strike of Hong Kong workers had taken place, crippling British Hong Kong and revealing in every step the unconquerable power of the working class and the historic role it was destined to play in the Chinese revolution. This strike had sent the first great chill of fear and hate through the Chinese ruling class and through the foreign imperialists who sat enthroned in the chief cities of our country. The strikers had spent their time during the strike building modern paved roads in and around Canton, until the city had taken on an entirely new aspect.

"Also throughout Kwangtung Province I found that millions of peasants had organized their Peasant Leagues and were throwing off the ancient feudal chains of landlordism and usury and the more modern shackles forged by militarists and officials. It was not the first time in Chinese history that peasants had revolted, but it was the first time in history that they had come under the leadership of a clearly revolutionary party with a social program for their emancipation. This party was the Chinese Communist Party, which had organized the workers and peasants and, two years before, had allied itself with the Kuomintang.

"Through such developments as these I had long since realized that my childhood dreams of leading an army to free the slaves were childhood dreams indeed. For here was a social system in the making, a system rising to free the vast laboring masses of China. The girl slaves that I had once longed to free were now regarded as human beings, and to buy or sell them was a criminal offense punishable by death; no longer did men have to sign away their lives to the plantations or in the mines of colonial slave-drivers.

"But at the same time, as I passed through Hong Kong and visited my family for a few hours, and as I now moved about Canton, I realized what a dangerous and fearful situation the revolution was facing. For the workers' and peasants' organizations were young and inadequately armed. And the feudal merchant class, the old officials, and all the bourgeois intellectuals that had sprung from their ranks were adopting every measure possible to regain their lost power and crush the rising mass revolution.

"I myself was a member of the Chinese Communist Party. Of my own free desire and under instructions from my party, I joined the medical corps attached to the army known as the Ironsides. With my hair cropped short and in military uniform, I was one of the women revolutionaries who marched from Canton to the Yangtze Valley.

"Those of us who have lived through the Great Chinese Revolution can never forget the released energies and hopes of the millions of hard-laboring peasants and workers. Half-naked, bent with the oppression of centuries, the peasants arose by the millions, straightened their backs, and began the work of emancipating themselves. They fought in the revolutionary army, they acted as guides, they stood by the hour along routes which the army took on its march, waiting with free food and drink for our forces. They began to cut down rent and usurious interest, to cancel all illegal taxes, and in many places to confiscate the land of big landlords and drive out the reactionary gentry. Apart from their direct aid to the revolutionary army, throughout South China there began great peasant struggles in which thousands fought hand-to-hand battles with old militarist forces, with landlords and the gentry. They did not wait for the revolutionary army to come; but with the news of our approach they began holding meetings, and then their fierce struggles against the forces of reaction began.

"The famous Ironsides to which I was attached became known more and more as a Communist Army. Among our commanding officers were a number of Communists who later remained true to their principles and are today to be found among the leaders of the Red worker-peasant armies of Central China. Our army was unconquerable, we covered ourselves with glory, and with the help of the masses nothing could stand against us. We were among those that captured Hankow and Hanyang, and we laid siege to Wuchang until it fell. My body was now strong and tough, and there seemed no limit to my ability to work, whether in the lazarettes or in carrying the wounded from the field after hard battles. With my hands I closed in death the eyes of hundreds of the most heroic youth of China. With each man or woman whom I watched die for the revolution, the deeper did the iron of conviction penetrate my being. The tears that used to flow from my eyes dried up, and in their place developed an energy that knew no end.

"Our army marched on to Nanchang, and it was while we were in Nanchang that the counter-revolution broke and the frightful White Terror began. The military officers within the ranks of the army were sons of landlords and of the gentry, or they sprang from the professional militarists or capitalists of the cities. From the first they had feared and hated the power of the workers and peasants, and as the masses emancipated themselves more and more these officers, together with the landlords, the gentry, the capitalists of the cities, united in one front to preserve the old order, to kill the new in birth.

"Within our army the officers especially hated the political councils which gave the common soldiers human rights. When the officers were forced to attend these weekly councils of soldiers and officers, common privates had the right to arise and demand from them explanations or accounts of expenditures of money; or to ask why the officers had not paid the wages that the soldiers were supposed to get. All the ancient corrupt privileges of the officers, by which they had made fortunes, were swept away.

"Finally the time came, as it had to come, when the forces of reaction and the forces of revolution came into open conflict. In Shanghai Chiang Kai-shek inaugurated the White Terror by a frightful massacre of workers and intellectuals. Then the Terror was let loose upon the peasants who had dared lift their heads and stand

upright. Hundreds of thousands of peasants and workers, badly armed and but newly organized, were
slaughtered. All the forces of feudal reaction were
unleashed and the soil of China ran red.

"But the revolutionary forces fought to preserve the
revolution. In Nanchang our uprising against the reaction failed; then, led by Communist officers of our
army, we marched through the entire length of Kiangsi
and made for Swatow, which we hoped to capture, and
then to Canton, which we hoped would again become
the bulwark of the revolution. But the revolution was
too young, the forces of the reaction, now actively
reënforced by the imperialists in the city, too strong. In
Swatow we fought and were defeated and in this
fighting I found it necessary to lay aside my medical kit
and take up a rifle. When we had reached South China, I
felt that I knew all the reaction was capable of doing,
for I was from the reactionary ruling class, the dealers in
human slaves, the dealers in opium. And although I did
my duty to the wounded, there were times when that
was no longer possible. I fought. And I fought with hard
hatred.

"Defeated—yes—temporarily. Our forces retreated,
separated. Some went into Fukien and Kiangsi. Some of
us made our way to Canton. Dressed as a lady of
fashion, I took up my residence in Canton. There were
times when I had wavered, thinking still that a united
front of the masses and the bourgeoisie might be
possible until the grip of the imperialists upon China
was broken. But the crushing of the Canton Commune
dealt the death-blow to the last lingering illusion in my
mind.

"On December 11, 1927, the workers and peasants of
Canton arose and with very little bloodshed established
the Canton Commune. A few soldiers, taking shelter in
the Central Bank, fought, and in driving them out the
Bank was destroyed by fire and some surrounding

buildings were burned. Then the Commune began the organization of a revolutionary worker-peasant government, the center for a new free society of the Chinese people.

"Three days later the reactionary troops, accompanied by a number of foreigners and led by some of the most feudal of Chinese officers, captured Canton. They were assisted by foreign gunboats lying at anchor in the Pearl River. The Commune was overthrown and the slaughter of the people began. Such scenes of carnage have perhaps been witnessed in past Chinese history when dynasties have been overthrown and new ones established, but certainly the slaughters of rebel peasant masses in past centuries and the slaughters of Genghis-Khan when he over-ran other countries could have been no more savage than that of the workers, peasants, and intellectuals of Canton by the White troops under the direction of feudal officers.

"Whole sections of the city were ruined by fire and fighting, and workingmen and women, student men and girls, were murdered by thousands in the streets. The White officers killed every workingman or student they met—sometimes they halted them, then shot them dead; or they had them captured, forced to their knees, and beheaded or sliced into bits. Every girl with bobbed hair who was caught was stripped naked, raped by as many men as were present, then her body slit in two, from below upwards. Often the girls were no more than fifteen or sixteen, and officers, giving interviews to eager British journalists from Hong Kong, said: 'The bobbed-haired girls are the worst; they are very arrogant and talk back defiantly. We have had to kill hundreds of them.'

"The bodies of the slaughtered were piled up like the carcasses of pigs. On one day alone four thousand prisoners were marched outside the city and mowed down with machine guns, in the presence of smiling officials of the foreign imperialist consular services, who posed to have their pictures taken against a background of corpses. Five officials of the Soviet Russian Consulate were arrested, marched through the streets, their pockets robbed of all the money they had, their shoes taken from their feet, and were then murdered. One woman of the consulate was murdered by impaling her on a huge stick driven through her body from the vagina.

"Four years later, in Shanghai, I listened in silence as the wife of an American military intelligence officer told of how this woman had been killed and showed a photograph she had of her, impaled. After this official's wife ceased speaking, she remarked self-righteously: 'But you know I have not the least sympathy with such a woman!' Then I knew, even if I had never known before, that the ruling class of the United States is no more humane than the feudal reaction of China, and that when the American workers one day begin their struggle to free themselves from the slavery of capitalism they will face a Terror just as fearful as anything we in China are facing.

"After days of slaughter in Canton the rich began to venture into the streets. I also went about, clad as a bourgeois lady in a gown of silk. As such I was safe. As a poor woman I would have been cut down. But now I walked about and saw wounded and dying workingmen in the streets, left as they had been cut or shot down. I saw bourgeois women go through the streets, bend over wounded and dying workingmen, and beat out their brains with chunks of stone or wood. All the humanity that is supposed to slumber in the well-bred breasts of women of the ruling class, whether of China or of other lands, was now revealed to me in all its horror. I heard from others that some such women took penknives and carved out souvenirs of flesh from the dead bodies of

the Soviet officials before these were dumped in the
mass trenches that furnish the last resting place of the
revolutionary martyrs of Canton.

"The régime of the bourgeoisie and the militarists was
reëstablished. All labor unions except the yellow
Mechanics Union, a semi-official union whose officers
had helped the reaction, were disbanded. The merchants
of the city, whose armed volunteer corps had been
dissolved by the revolutionary government and even by
Dr. Sun Yat-sen years before, now reorganized and
heavily armed it. The Peasant Leagues throughout the
province were smashed and thousands of peasants killed
in the struggle.

"And now all the old feudal-capitalist order of
Canton was reëstablished. Opium dens flourished, and
opium became one of the chief articles of sale, import
and export; gambling, banquets, prostitutes again became the chief amusement of the officials. The traffic in
girl slaves again flourished and in the months that
followed I was again personal witness to the buying and
selling of girls from the peasantry into the homes of the
merchants and official classes, as household drudges, as
concubines.

"The new régime then returned also to the ancient
system of robbery and taxation of the peasants; it
auctioned off to the highest bidders the right of
collection of taxes from the peasantry. These bidders
would offer millions of dollars to the government for
such rights. Then, with their own armed forces, they
were turned loose upon the peasants to levy and collect
taxes. They paid the government what they were
pledged to pay; all surplus they kept for themselves. The
new government placed no restrictions upon the extent
of this surplus. Like vultures, these private taxation
vampires bled the peasants white. All the human rights
the Peasant Leagues had won, all the hopes and dreams

of the peasants, were crushed by the newly established régime of merchants, politicians and militarists. Like clouds of locusts these settled over Kwangtung and all China.

"I have seen the face of the Chinese ruling class; which means I have seen the face of the ruling class of imperialist countries also. For in the reëstablishment of the reaction in China they have worked together like the blood brothers that they are. There is no atrocity, no brutality, no crime against human beings of which they are not capable. This class has nothing to offer China—nothing but debased destitution, nothing but slavery, nothing but corruption and final subjection.

"Of course I am a Communist. What else can any person be who desires that the vast masses of toiling human beings shall become free men, developing for themselves a culture such as has been denied them through all ages? As a convinced Communist I am working in the ranks of the revolutionary workers and peasants of Central China, where we have established a Chinese Soviet Government, where we are laying the foundations for a human, a free Communist society. In this territory I am a physician, a public health worker; and all that it was my privilege to learn as a member of the privileged classes I have now placed at the disposal of the peasants and workers.

"We started with nothing but the ancient system of brutal ignorance and subjection; today we have schools, hospitals, clubs, dramatic societies—as also free land for all that labor, and our varied political and military defense organs. In this territory I travel far and wide, establishing health institutes, lecturing on public health and hygiene, teaching women the care of themselves and their children. I have looked so long into the eager faces of millions of the oppressed, thirsty for knowledge, that now my eyes can see nothing else. When, for one reason or another that I am not free to state, I am compelled to make trips to the cities of brutal reaction, like Shanghai, these eager faces are always before me, calling.

"As for my old feudal family, the family into which I was born—they are to me but a dark and ugly memory, and to them I am but a fearful dream. My hope is that if I ever face them and their kind it will be as a part of the Red Army, to destroy all that they value, to bring to human existence those whom they enslave. They once tried to pin me to a marriage bed with a millionaire that I might breed more creatures like themselves. But I chose a man I loved from the ranks of the revolution, and for permission to live with him I asked no priest or policeman whose blessings give sanctity to bourgeois marriages. My husband fell before the Terror, and although my heart lies with him in his nameless, unknown grave in Hankow, still he died heroically for the masses of our country, and his death has but steeled me for further unceasing labor.

"You wished to know the rôle I play in China. It is enough to say that I am a Communist, for that means I am fighting in the ranks for a new world. It means that I may one day cease to appear on this stage of historical events—but it means also that all that I work for now will be carried to fruition by the revolution of which I am but a part. Now I will be on my way, for there is much to do and I never know how much longer I have to do the share allotted to me."

FIVE WOMEN OF MUKDEN

It is night here within these great Manchu walls of Mukden. The life of the International Settlement and the Japanese Concession on the outside, and the life and ideas of China to the south, seem thousands of miles away. At midnight when the four steel-studded gates of the walls swing shut, to be opened only at five in the morning, the world beyond seems more distant still. And it is indeed, for many decades of thought and action lie between Chinese Mukden and the outside world.

The moon is very white, and the cold seems to have frozen up all sound. All except the long, weird cry of a

New Republic, June 11, 1930, pp. 99-101. Mukden (now called Shen-yang) was the capital of Manchuria, which by 1930 was a semi-colony of Japan. Chang Hsüeh-liang was a local warlord who was nominally attached to the Kuomintang government of Chiang Kai-shek. Later, in 1936, Chang would kidnap Chiang at Sian (see introduction).

beggar woman standing outside our little stone garden gate. She cries again and again, "Blessings upon your home . . . may you become rich. . . ." And when at last not one of the little gray houses within our compound will give her bread, she goes away. After she is gone the only sound in the garden is the rustling of the dried leaves of the tall kaoliang stalks piled high against the gray stone walls.

Inside our house a little Chinese woman is talking—of her husband, of policemen, of debts, of the so-called courts and of Marshal Chang Hsueh-liang, whose fortified castle rears its feudal heights in the moonlight but two streets from us. If you walk there, you will see only the bleak face of a great stone wall twenty feet high, and gray-clad soldiers with fixed guns to challenge you.

The little woman talking is still young, and her soft black hair is drawn back and rolled into a knot at the back of her neck. In her face and her quick, watchful black eyes lies a strange expression. "She is very beautiful," I say to my Chinese friends. "No, she is not beautiful," one of them replies; then, as if caught by another thought, he corrects himself, "Yes, she is . . . but not the type considered beautiful." Perhaps long association with a husband who is fifty years in advance of the times in Manchuria has left on her face an expression of swift intelligence, long watchful endurance, and a composure that comes when one has passed beyond tears. She sits very quietly, her folded hands in her lap, and tells of her husband. Nine months ago his friend was arrested in Kirin to the north. Under torture this friend admitted that he was a member of the Kuomintang, and that her husband in Mukden was also a member. Then her husband was arrested as a "Communist." His fate was better than that of the many others who have simply disappeared from the sight of man. There was no proof against him except the word of the tortured man—that and his record of many years' service in social activities such as famine-relief work in Shantung. But "proof" is a new-fangled idea that no official in Manchuria worries about.

To save her husband from torture and death, this little woman with the beautiful face went to friends, and together they borrowed enough money to bribe the officials and jailors. They continue to borrow and bribe; the avarice of the officials is as deep as eternity. And now that the new Nanking penal code is said to be in force—and who is to interpret it but the old and corrupt officials or the new reactionary ones?—they have had to borrow six hundred American dollars to induce a lawyer to demand a trial for the husband. The law says "public trial," according to the new penal code. I naively remark that I wish to attend it. In the room about me there is shocked protest:

"If you do that, we shall all be arrested as Communists. . . . the trials are always secret . . . they will ask you what interest you have in this and where you heard of it."

Then the little woman with a beautiful face goes away, bowing gently with a "*zai jhen*," but her face shows that her thoughts are not with us. When she is gone there is again no sound except the rustling of the dry kaoliang leaves in our garden.

My hostess is a little old-fashioned Chinese lady in trousers and a short jacket. She is very frail, worn out from child-bearing—twelve children, of whom six are dead. When her husband enters the room, she rises and gives him her seat. She cannot read and she never goes out. Her eyes are very bright and intelligent and she sits for hours asking questions about the women of other lands. They are intelligent questions, such as modern

educated women might ask. She often sighs and is silent,
thinking of things strange to me. The women of the
West are very fortunate, she says; they can make their
own living and have children only when they wish. She
does not know of the modern women of her own
country to the south. How could she, having come here
from Chihli Province as a girl of fifteen, married to a
man she had never seen? Time and suffering are long,
Mukden is far from her old home, and her life has been
only bearing and burying children.

Now she is old, worn out and ugly, and her husband
is planning to buy a sing-song girl of sixteen and bring
her home as his second wife. My little hostess does not
dare object. But her eldest son is a modern student in
long black flowing robes, and he objects. He has told his
father that he leaves home, never to return, the day he
takes a second wife.

"You are a son . . . you will act like a son!" his father
informs him.

But the son is impious and clear-minded, and a week
ago his father struck him across the face. They say
Chinese sons love their fathers. Not the sons I have
known. Never have I seen more hatred in the eyes of a
man than in those of this eldest son of my hostess. He
speaks little before a guest, but his eyes speak when
they light on his father. There is constant friction
between them.

"In the olden days," the father boasts to me, "the
daughter-in-law had to stand while the son's parents
ate."

The son breaks in: "That is the reason so many of
them died!"

"Hold your tongue, you silly thing!" the father
commands.

But the son does not hold his tongue, and the father
dares bring home no second wife.

A young woman teacher, in a long blue cotton tunic and with hair cut like a boy's, sits talking. She is a returned student from America. We had tried to get inside the women's prison in Mukden. To this young woman the director said:

"Tell the foreign woman the director is ill and nothing can be done without his permission." Then he said, for her own private information: "No, she may not visit the prison. It is not clean enough for a foreign journalist to see."

This teacher, however, may visit the prison, for she is a Chinese and goes in as a welfare worker. The women of Manchuria are still half-slaves, she tells me. Men still have many wives and concubines. The women have no rights over their own lives. The very idea of a divorce is considered immoral. A man may "put away" his wife, or bring in concubines, but his first wife may not object. She must even pretend to be a friend of the newcomer.

"What are the crimes the women prisoners here are charged with?" I asked. "Murder," the young woman teacher replies. "The majority are in for murder."

"Murder! . . . why . . . what?"

"Their husbands," she answers.

Some women are passive and some are not, and I saw one who was thought to be passive. She was a miserable looking, foot-bound peasant woman, an immigrant from Shantung begging in the streets. Hobbling along on her tiny feet over the frozen street, she slipped and fell, and landed sitting, sprawled out in the middle of the chief street of the city. A small bag of bread burst and scattered in every direction. A little child in rags stood by her side helplessly.

The street was filled with men who saw the accident. Not one came forward to help. Instead they began to laugh, and the policeman on the corner watched and laughed with them. Three young fops, dressed in flowered silk gowns, formal smart little black jackets and tight round black silk caps, joined a crowd that gathered. All laughed.

The peasant woman did not move a leg. But she braced herself with her hands and surveyed the crowd, back and forth and all around, as a general might survey a battlefield. Then she began. She cursed the assembled men, all their ancestors back to the thousandth generation, and all the brats they would bring into the world in the future. She cursed them individually and collectively, up and down and around and about. She cursed systematically and thoroughly, working them over inch by inch. Under her words the laughter froze up on the faces of the men, as if a sudden blast of Siberian weather had struck them. They began to hurry away, and it may have been my imagination that made some of them seem half-paralyzed. But, as they rushed away or crawled away in astonishment, the voice of the peasant woman followed them with her highest compliments. New and perfectly innocent men turned the corner and, seeing her sitting there, also began to laugh. But deliberately she turned her tongue on them and like a cat-o'-nine-tails it seemed to lash all laughter out of them. Their faces froze up and they also hurried past as fast as their feet could carry them. And at last the street was almost clear.

Then, with infinite trouble and in misery, the peasant woman managed to scramble to her tiny pin-like feet again. The child, who had been standing by throughout, helped her, gathered up the bread, and the two of them hobbled out of sight.

The streets are filled with men, but few women. Occasionally automobiles or rickshas carrying exquisitely dressed ladies pass. Some of these ladies are smoking cigarettes or small pipes. Now and again two or three modern girls swing past, their hair cut short, their hands in their pockets, their feet big and their minds free. It is easy to see that they are students, free of gait and manner, self-confident and proud.

Once in a tramway a student girl dressed in the usual blue cotton gown got in with an older woman. Clearly they were mother and daughter. Many decades of culture lay between them. The mother had bound feet and long hair done into a smooth, glistening roll at the back of her neck. The girl was as strong and tall as a northern Chinese man, with short hair, natural feet and an intelligent and self-confident face.

The tram was filled with men and not one place was vacant. The girl grasped the wooden rod above with one hand and supported her old mother with the other. The only person in the whole car of fifty or more men to rise and offer a seat to the old lady was a young man who, by his dress, was obviously a student. The old lady was surprised into an outburst of gratitude. The other men passengers watched the student in amusement, spat, and laughed outright that a man could be so weak. The student and the tall girl both turned on them a look of withering scorn. Two of them—among fifty. The percentage is too low for south China, but far too high for Manchuria.

HSU
MEI-LING

Hsu Mei-Ling was an old-fashioned girl, with all the faults and virtues of an old-fashioned girl. She was brought up in the old-fashioned way—taught reading, painting and embroidery on silk, household management, and how to write beautiful characters. She is now thirty, the mother of four children. She is still young, attractive, and she has the delicate, fair skin so common to Chinese women who are not factory workers or peasants. Her glossy black hair was formerly drawn back from a lovely forehead and coiled softly at the base of her neck, and in the coil she often wore a cluster of sweet-smelling blossoms. Her high-throated silk Chinese gown, without one touch of decoration and without one break in the line, fell to the ankle in chaste beauty,

New Republic, April 9, 1930, pp. 219-20. An earlier version of this story appeared in German as "Das Schicksal von Hsü Mei-ling," *Frankfurter Zeitung*, December 25, 1929.

softly suggesting her slender body. And her feet were always encased in soft heelless shoes.

She is very graceful—until she walks. Then she is stiff and awkward, and if you look closely you can see the broad bands beneath her stockings. Her ankles are bound. Formerly, when a little girl in interior China, her feet had been tightly bound and crippled. But then came the anti-foot-binding movement, and the revolution, and all women under thirty were urged to free their feet. The women's associations in south and central China sent emissaries from door to door to agitate against foot-binding and long hair; there were cases where conservative, superstitious women refused, and the modern women took the law into their own hands, cut their hair and unbound their feet by force.

Hsu Mei-ling unbound her feet, enduring torture as great as when they were bound, a torture that gave rise to the old proverb, "a small foot and an ocean of tears." But even though unbound, her feet will always be crippled, and now she must wear them half-bound.

Mei-ling is five years older than her husband. Her husband graduated from an American mission school and then a mission college. He is one of the worshipers of modernity, which he confuses with Americanism. He knows American songs, history and literature, and he can write better English than Chinese. He speaks English through his nose. His one dream is to go to the Ford factory in America and then return to China as an agent for Ford automobiles. But since he has not money to do this, he is a clerk in a bank in Shanghai. For some insane reason he removed Mei-ling and the children from the interior to Shanghai also, and he set about to make his wife as modern as himself.

The old rambling Chinese houses, with their colored tiled roofs, their lovely filigree windows, and the carved Chinese furniture of curious design, he regarded as symbols of things to be destroyed. He is a modern man.

So he rented a small, modern flat where the windows are very square and the walls very blank and white, and where the brilliant electric lights are made more glaring still by white enamel lampshades such as Western people have in their bathrooms. This house he furnished with cheap upholstered furniture and with knickknacks such as missionary houses often have. Instead of old Chinese scrolls with philosophic sayings or long panel-like paintings of delicate pines and bamboos, he bought modern, gaudily colored prints of moonlight on German and Swiss landscapes. These he framed in broad, golden frames and they hang on his walls. But the picture he treasures most is a huge photograph of the Grand Central Station in New York City. Then he added his final touch—a phonograph with many American jazz records. One of his little daughters, just eight, can dance the Charleston exceedingly well. This has been a blessing, and he has been generous in that he did not force Mei-ling to follow the habit of women missionaries in China and wear a foreign hat turned up in the back like a duck's tail.

Mei-ling moves about in this strange, ugly flat like a ghost over some long-forgotten Chinese battlefield. She is old-fashioned, loving the old things of China. Her whole being breathes the reserve, the dignity and the composure of the old-fashioned girl. But she is also ignorant, superstitious and suspicious, and understands only one relationship between men and women. The Shanghai setting has come upon her like a disaster. Her husband talks modernity night and day—and is it not a virtue for the wife always to bow to the will of the husband? So she accepted the house, the jazz records, and she used to go to the cinemas two or three times a week with him. She looked at the film posters, all of which seemed to show men lying on women's bodies, or about to do so, and in horror she watched the films that showed these foreign women in low-necked gowns, embracing men and kissing them shamelessly. All the films seemed to show either a willing or an unwilling woman in this role. Even the growing dissatisfaction and impatience of her husband failed to overcome her shrinking before such things. So more and more her husband left her alone with the children and spent his evenings with his friends.

Then came the affair with the white-guard Russian dancing girl. She is a doll-faced, curly-haired dancing girl in a Shanghai night café. When Hsu Mei-ling first learned of her, she would throw herself on her husband's coat and lie weeping desperately, clasping it in her arms to prevent him from going out in the evening. "Hsu Mei-ling is jealous," the friends of her husband said, laughing knowingly. "She is an old-fashioned girl. She is also old." For in China people still think that a woman of thirty is old.

Mei-ling could speak but little English, and even had she spoken fluently, she would never have exposed her heart to the gaze of friends. But her husband was as modern and as empty as most clerks, and any idea or trouble that entered his soul made a noise as loud as a pea in an empty gourd. "I did not marry her because I wanted to," he once exclaimed bitterly about Mei-ling. "She is ignorant and old-fashioned and can get no idea in her head. I can get no help from her and I am going to put her away."

"To put her away is old-fashioned," I argued. "And then, what about the children?"

"That is not my fault! She likes children. She can take them and go to my parents. She can have all the property I have there."

"And this Russian girl. . . ?"

"She is modern and she would never prevent me from rising. She wants to go to America also."

"Perhaps she loves you because she wants to go to America."

I knew nothing of the girl, he argued. But he was wrong. For once Hsu Mei-ling had taken me to the café where the girl dances. One did not have to know her personally to know what kind of girl she was. But Mei-ling hoped to see her and to know the life that had captured her husband. We entered the café and sat at a table. Mei-ling sat gingerly on the edge of the chair while her eyes scanned the gaudy hall. Her eyes are very black and penetrating, and it is possible that such eyes see more than do the eyes of modern women. They studied each girl on the floor, her dress, face and feet. Mei-ling's face was expressionless in its intensity, but the eyes were like fire. A Chinese jazz orchestra beat out the rhythm of "Sonya" and at the proper moment bellowed out:

I'm heart-sick and sore
Because you love your Nikolaus no more!

The days had passed as usual after this, with Mei-ling's husband more and more determined to "put her away." The weeping increased, the conflicts increased, his absences from home increased. Then Mei-ling ceased weeping. One day she appeared with bobbed hair, and a short time afterwards she had it waved. The chaste simplicity and dignity that had given her distinction before now vanished, and she appeared a miserable woman trying to compete with an empty-headed dancing girl for an empty-headed husband. It was not long after this that I called, and when she came into the room I saw that her long, graceful gown had been shortened almost to the knees, like those which modern Chinese girls wear. Below were her heavy, awkward ankles, tightly wrapped with bandages, which one had not noticed before unless she walked.

On this day she turned on the phonograph and, lifting her wistful, miserable face, shyly entreated, "Teach me to dance." The phonograph began to shriek through the strains of a record. She had even bought the record we heard that evening in the café.

But to dance, there must be joy in the heart and the feet must be elastic and light. And Mei-ling's heart was as heavy as lead and her feet had been crippled while she was still a child. After taking a few lame steps, she stopped suddenly in the middle of the floor and wept like a little girl, holding the sleeve of her gown before her face. Two of the children stood in the doorway watching their mother. Their eyes were big with wonder. Behind us the phonograph yelped out:

> *'Twas in November and my heart was full of vodka*
> *Yup! Alay Yup!*
> *That's when I'm thinking of you, Sonya!*

THE LIV- ING DEAD

I

In Nanking there is an old and spacious Chinese home, the home of one of the highest officials in the Government, a man known as a scholar and statesman. His title to scholarship rests on his ability to write handsome scrolls embodying ancient proverbs of the feudal past; his statesmanship rests upon his willingness to act as apologist for the militarists in power. Thereto he is very old, and with those who think in terms of the ancient past his age is supposed to lend weight to all he says or does.

In his home live nine women; of these eight are concubines and one his daughter. And through the halls of the home and even in the enclosed garden where the

Chinese Destinies: Sketches of Present-Day China, pp. 97-108. For background on 1927, the year of the bloody purge of Communists by Chiang Kai-shek, see the editors' introduction.

women wander, hangs always the sweetish, sickening odor of opium. For all the concubines smoke opium. And now the daughter also.

This daughter, whose name is Chi-yueh, did not always smoke opium, did not always wander through these drug-soaked rooms and enclosed garden like a disembodied soul. For once she was a revolutionist—a Communist—and waged war on opium, on concubinage, and on all the decadent old ideas that recognize age or calligraphy as statesmanship or scholarship. That was over five years ago when she, a tall, vital girl, in military uniform, marched with the revolutionary army from Canton to the Yangtze. Now she is a woman in lovely, flowered silk gowns that fall from her shoulders to her ankles over a form so emaciated that it resembles a formless bamboo.

In was in the days of the great mass revolution, that is, from the years 1922 to 1927, that this girl went with her young husband to Moscow to study. The husband, a man with a mind as sharp as a sword, was the son of a poor scholar's family in Nanchang, Kiangsi, and was one of the early members of the Chinese Communist Party. Chi-yueh, young, beautiful, and idealistic, followed him not merely in body, but in mind also, as most Chinese women follow their husbands. In Moscow she studied a lesson that most Chinese women, including even the Communists, have yet to learn—that a woman, like a man, is an independent personality, a productive force destined to choose her own way regardless of family, father, husband. This Chi-yueh learned—in theory.

In 1926 she and her husband returned to China, filled with the fire of the new world in birth, filled with boundless love for each other, and above all determined to fight and live for the emancipation of the Chinese masses. They went immediately to Canton, the mecca of the revolution, and marched with the army to the

Wuhan cities, blending with the vast revolutionary movement that swept all the South. It was easy to be a revolutionist in those days, especially for Chi-yueh, surrounded by millions of revolutionists and with her husband, a peasant organizer, by her side.

But the fateful year of 1927 came. The counter-revolution began and the soil of the country ran red with the blood of workers, peasants, and intellectuals such as Chi-yueh and her husband. Chi-yueh's father was in the ranks of the counter-revolution and became one of the founders of the Nanking Government. As a feudal-minded man who hated the communists, perhaps because they challenged all that constituted his existence, he was one of the spokesmen for that Government.

In the fearful struggle that carried off tens of thousands of revolutionists, Chi-yueh's husband, fighting with the peasants, escaped capture and death. But one day in Kiukiang on the Yangtze a bobbed-haired girl was arrested, accused of being a Communist, and after a few seconds' examination before a military tribunal, condemned to death. The court—for such it was called—stayed its hand only because the girl declared that she was the daughter of the old feudal scholar in Nanking. The sentence of death was suspended until her statement could be tested, and when the answer came that she spoke the truth her sentence was suspended indefinitely.

The old man came to Kiukiang and faced his daughter in prison, under sentence of death. And since everything in China is determined by personal issues, the sentence was rescinded at his request. But then began Chi-yueh's struggle, which was more terrible than fighting the Terror. Removed from the presence of the revolution and of her husband, who had always before stood by her side, this girl faced alone all the feudal influences in which she had been reared.

Each day her father came and pleaded with her, often with tears and sometimes upon his knees. He was her father, he was old, she was his only child. It was he who had given her existence; in love he had brought her to life, fed her, clothed her, educated her even when girls in his family were not educated. She was his daughter, her life belonged to him. He asked that she give her word to leave the Communist Party, that she pledge, publicly, never to participate in revolutionary work again.

This pleading was accompanied by other developments. Chi-yueh was taken from the filthy, dark, damp prison in which others of her comrades awaited death. From this atmosphere she was removed to one of the warden's comfortable private rooms where she was held prisoner and where her father visited her daily. In this atmosphere and through his pleadings, Chi-yueh still heard the distant voices of her comrades, and she fought off his influence. Then he had her removed to the prison in Soochow, where she was given a special room furnished with every possible comfort. Here she was to remain until she changed her attitude and did as her father wished. And to this end the old man visited her often, coming from Nanking but a short distance away.

The weeks and even months wore on. The voices of Chi-yueh's comrades and the memories of their watchful eyes became more distant; and gradually they faded. When she thought of the freedom and safety outside and then of the possibility of going to join her comrades within a few yards from the room she occupied, her mind was appalled. Her father's voice grew more and more welcome. And at last the day came when she agreed to do as he asked.

When she was set at liberty she published a statement in the press that she had been a Communist, but that henceforth she severed all connections with the party or

its activities. Then she accompanied her father to Nanking and took up her abode in the home where his
concubines lived.

Her husband, the peasant organizer, read her statement in the press. No one knows what it meant to him,
but it is known that he had loved her with overpowering
love and had been proud that she was a revolutionary
woman. Still, he knew Chinese women, their strength
and weaknesses, he knew the ties which bind them to
their families, to old ideas, and to institutions of the
dark past; for he was a Chinese and himself had come
from this old and decadent society.

After she had bought her freedom, Chi-yueh received
one letter from her husband—one and one only. It was
short and very clear; it was signed, not by the intimate
name by which she had known him, but by the full,
formal name he used officially. The letter told her she
had betrayed the revolution, betrayed Communism
which alone is worth living or dying for; she had purchased her freedom and her life that now became worthless and repulsive. This she had done at a moment when
the Chinese masses were standing at the crossroads of
their existence, facing either emancipation or continued
servitude. With the merciless bitterness that springs from
disappointed love and with the hardness that springs
from unwavering conviction, he branded her as a traitor
to the revolution, a traitor to the masses of her country,
a woman dead to him forever. The letter contained not
one breath of tenderness or regret, but only a curt and
final farewell. And only this much Chi-yueh knew of
him after that: he went into Kiangsi, attached himself to
the Red Army, and became one of those who helped
found the Chinese Soviet Government.

Chi-yueh lives in the home of her father in Nanking,
and she has had five years in which to contemplate the
value of life bought as she bought hers. Five years—not
of contemplation but of dreams; and these dreams are

such as come from opium. Her husband's one letter has lain beneath her pillow for five years, and on this pillow she has rested her head as she smokes and dreams. No sign of his existence has since reached her by letter. But now and then an official newspaper report mentions his name, calling him one of the "bandit" leaders fighting for the workers and peasants of Central China.

Chi-yueh reads such a report, then sinks back on her pillow and smokes. Her body, once strong and vigorous, has become emaciated; her once glowing face is now the color of white paper; and her eyes are sunken like those of an old woman. A ghost of a woman, she wanders in silence in the enclosed garden of her father's home or pauses to exchange idle gossip with his concubines.

Between the living past and the dead present she has built a bridge of opium dreams, and what they are she and she alone knows. Or, it may be, the fumes of opium have even killed the memories of the past.

II

In Nanking there wanders also another woman from the ranks of the revolution of former days. Kuo-nan she is called, and she and her husband also studied in Moscow. Returning to China in April, 1927, at the beginning of the counter-revolution and the mass slaughters in Shanghai, hardly had they set foot on the soil of that city than her husband was seized by the British police, turned over to the Chinese reaction, marched to the execution ground with over one hundred other men and women, and beheaded. His body was thrown like the carcass of an animal in the mass graves, as long and deep as war trenches, in which the bodies of revolutionary youth were hurled.

When Kuo-nan learned of this execution, something went wrong with her mind. She did not cry as other women do, but with hard dry eyes, she began to talk ceaselessly, everywhere. She told and retold in a thousand forms the life of her husband, the way he was butchered, the way he died.

"They made him kneel, they tied his hands behind him . . . but he cried 'Long live Communism! Long live the Revolution!' . . . For he was a Communist, and I am a Communist Youth."

Thus she talked, endlessly. If her friends left the room while she was speaking, she would rise and follow on their heels, saying: "They bound his hands and made him kneel before they chopped off his head, but he cried 'Long live Communism! Long live the Revolution!' For he was a Communist—and I am a Communist Youth!"

At first her friends would never leave her by herself, for she struck terror to their hearts lest her talking bring disaster upon them. For a long time they would induce her to remain indoors or in her room. But if they tried to lock her door, she would look at them and cynically remark: "You think I am insane, don't you? You are trying to lock me in! Because my husband has been killed and I am a Communist Youth!" And lest she become totally insane, they would comfort her and unlock the door and leave her at liberty. Then as the weeks passed she would wander the city, going from the home of one friend to another, talking, talking, talking. With hard, shining eyes she forced all to listen to the life and butchery of her husband. Some would say: "She is mad. Be careful that she does not talk before enemies."

But Kuo-nan never talked before enemies. She knew no foreigners, and, as if guided by instinct, she remained silent in the presence of Chinese strangers, only listening in tense silence to every word they uttered, sitting on the edge of her chair as if ready to leap upon them.

Many months passed and she ceased talking. She wandered to Nanking, and one day appeared at Kuomintang headquarters and said to an official: "Now, you have killed my husband. So you must kill me also, for he was a Communist and I am a Communist Youth. I am not active and so I am fit for nothing. So either kill me, or give me work that I may pass my worthless life. Give me figures to add all day long, that I may not think." For some reason or other the official placed her in a separate room and gave her mechanical work to do, paying her thirty dollars a month; for it was clear that she was deranged and was hardly worth a bullet.

Now Kuo-nan has sat in Nanking for five years, a woman who looks neither to the right nor to the left, who never reads, seeks recreation, or visits friends. In the early morning she goes to work, and at night she returns to her little room, bare in its austerity; she cooks some food on a primus stove and goes to bed. So her life is spent. On the small table by her bed rests a photograph, of postal-card size, encased in a cheap, dark frame. Out of this frame gazes a thin young man, perhaps twenty-five years old, of eager, serious expression. In the morning, and at night before going to bed, Kuo-nan sits looking silently into the face of this man, her dead husband.

Sometimes a friend of former days calls on her—friends who have betrayed the revolution and become officials. Kuo-nan greets them with the naïve directness that shocks and induces them to leave her in peace thereafter. She says: "I am a Communist Youth, although I am not active. If I were active I would not be here and I would not be talking to such as you!"

When these friends angrily denounce her to the official responsible for her, he will reply: "She is a mad woman and can do no harm. If I thought she could—" He leaves the threat unfinished.

Thus five years have passed in the living grave of Nanking for the wife of a revolutionary whose dust has blended with that of the ever new martyrs in the mass graves of Shanghai.

III

Hsi-chen claims that in the days of the great revolution she was a "C.Y.," or Communist Youth. But that is a matter on which opinions differ. For even when she went to study in Moscow, those who knew her denied that she was a "C.Y." She was a superficial girl with an empty, baby face, they said, who spent her time lolling on a bed with her lover.

This lover was, indeed, a Communist, and a prominent one—one of the founders of the Chinese Communist Party; and it was perhaps his personal influence that enabled Hsi-chen to go to Moscow in the first place. Of study she did little; when not posing as a modern woman, she cuddled up against her lover and twittered baby-talk to him in the manner of so many rich or middle-class women. Such manners are supposed to make women "cute" and attractive to men. Hsi-chen wore the title "C.Y." because her lover was a Communist, much as some college girls in the West wear the fraternity pins of their lovers. And he, a man already advanced in years, with ideas of woman formed in his dark, feudal youth, considered it wonderful indeed that a woman could be a "C.Y." and still be unable to exist without clinging to his own strong frame!

But when the counter-revolution began, it required no inducement to cause Hsi-chen to drop her title or any claim to it. With her class it was no longer the style. After much hesitation and maneuvering, her lover also went into the camp of the reaction and became one of the right-hand men of Chiang Kai-shek. For a long time there was a strange rumor about him; many said he still remained a Communist and had been secretly ordered by his party to do as he was doing. But if this were ever true, even in the first years of the terror, it was not true later on; for it was not to his liking to give up power, comfort, position and wealth for the life of a revolutionist whose every step may lead to death—or to worse than death: to torture. His service to the counter-revolution became a habit to which he became addicted, and he would not abandon it.

Hsi-chen lived secretly with this man for some time, then married him and went to live in a fine residence in Nanking. There in his home she received and entertained militarists and their wives who journeyed to the capital month in and month out. And although the years piled themselves one on the other, still she continued the empty-faced woman, twittering baby-talk to her husband even in the presence of others, pretending to be child-like and helpless in a clinging way.

But child-like, helpless or clinging though she may appear in the presence of her husband, there are times when such mannerisms fall from her. Such times are when she steps forward as a high and mighty lady of society, when she faces rivals over a gambling table, or when she meets friends of former days whom she suspects of having remained Communists.

As a high society lady, the wife of an official, Hsi-chen "lends her name" to "worthy causes," such as patriotic collections of money of which nothing is heard thereafter, the patronage of an occasional school, kindergarten or orphanage, or a charity performance. At such moments, stepping from her private car, attended by a man in military uniform or perhaps by one wearing an official badge, she delivers a speech of "encouragement" to the cause which she sponsors and for which she has perhaps given the munificent sum of fifty or one hundred dollars.

But she is seen at her best during the military conferences in Nanking when militarists or officials gather there, seeking money, power, higher positions. At such conferences Hsi-chen's home is turned into a guesthouse for those militarists and their wives who are not yet full-fledged henchmen of Chiang Kai-shek. Since gambling is the prime form of amusement of Hsi-chen and others of her class, every afternoon and evening the main rooms of her home are cleared for mah-jong tables, and here the wives of militarists and of the highest officials in the government feverishly gamble, losing and winning thousands of dollars. The clatter of mah-jong cubes can be heard even beyond the high enclosing walls of the building.

Over the gambling tables Hsi-chen is no longer a child-like, clinging creature but a mature woman, one of the most accomplished gamblers in Nanking. But still she does not always win—for to lose or to win is high politics. If Hsi-chen's rival happens to be the wife of a doubtful militarist, it is this woman who wins and it is Hsi-chen who makes stupid plays. And whatever the women may think under their breaths, still when the wife of such a militarist enters the room, gambling ceases as Hsi-chen rapturously exclaims:

"Oh, what an exquisite gown you have on today— what marvelous shoes! . . . And you have a new ring— jade surrounded by pearls! Five hundred dollars, you say? Of course, it costs quite a lot, but still if one wishes such lovely things one must not merely pay well for them but must have the good taste with which to choose them!"

The gambling parties cease long enough for tea and later again in the evening for the banquet with countless courses of expensive dishes. Hsi-chen is the perfect hostess, hardly deigning to lift a rice grain to her rose-bud mouth, repeatedly offering to serve the guests at her table. And the assembled ladies are themselves so elegant that they hardly taste of the dishes placed before them, and if they do show such low taste as the necessity for food their chop-sticks lift but tiny bits to their hard, calculating, painted faces.

The gambling continues after the banquet and lasts until the small hours of morning. The men return from

their conferences on how to fight down the revolutionary Red Army, from their banquets and parties with
sing-song girls who have been brought from high-class
houses or apartments in Shanghai, and who are paid
thousands of dollars a week for their "services." These
girls are especially placed at the disposal of the doubtful
militarists.

The wives of the militarists do not rise until afternoon, and then only to prepare for more gambling
parties. Generally Hsi-chen's home is one ceaseless
round of these parties, but sometimes the ladies are
taken on short automobile trips beyond the city walls,
or they commandeer the pleasure boats on Lotus Lake
and, reclining at ease, are rowed languidly over the
waters. At such times all boats are taken and no other
person permitted on the lake.

Hsi-chen is a mature, calculating woman at other
times also. Her past life among Chinese Communists in
Moscow and China has fitted her for a certain kind of
activity. She knows the names and faces of men and
women who were her former comrades and who have
not betrayed. For such men she watches, in Shanghai or
Nanking, and all she learns she repeats to her husband
and to his master. There are times when she accidentally
meets a man or a woman of whom she is not certain, or
whom her husband or his master suspect of retaining
their former allegiance. Such a man or woman she gra-
ciously invites to tea at her home and attempts to form
a friendship. To such a man or woman she will exclaim
happily:

"We were C.Y.'s together, weren't we? Such interesting days! I still retain my sympathies and I do not think
we were wrong!"

She is never so crude as to ask her guest what he or
she thinks now, but with all the indirectness and cunning of which a woman of her kind is capable she directs
the conversation so that an answer appears essential.

There are guests who are her equals in cunning, and thereto possess intelligence of which she knows nothing. This she instinctively feels, and such guests she watches with her round, black, lidless eyes that, like the eyes of a snake, do not even blink as she awaits their answers to her innuendoes.

Sometimes she offers to rescue this or that man or woman, captured in the net of the Terror and awaiting death; and to those who accept or seek her assistance she appears kind and confidential, sympathetic and generous. Sad indeed is this case, she says. Who was this man, what was he doing, who are his friends and family—where are they living? Her eyes watch the face of the guest.

As her husband or his master direct, she listens and watches everywhere, then returns to tell what she has learned. It is this she has heard of the Communists, it is that she has learned of their plans. This man is suspicious: once he was in Moscow, but now he holds a respectable position; he talks little and appears to know much. Or here is a suspicious woman: she dresses in cheap clothing, scorns paint and powder, does not gamble—and knows too much. These people must be Communists!

Those at whom her dainty white hand with its jade bracelet is directed may save themselves as best they can. If captured, there is the torture rack, the executioner's knife, the firing squad, or a living death in a dark, feudal prison. But for such as Hsi-chen there is wealth, power, position.

In Shanghai foreigners entertain her as the "charming wife of a good, strong man." But in Nanking this twittering lady cannot even hear the cock crow thrice in the dawn; for the sound of the crowing is drowned by the clatter of mah-jong cubes in her dreams, or the crack of rifles taking their toll of her former comrades.

THE STORY OF KWEI CHU

When I had finished telling my professor friend in Peking the story of Kwei Chu, he declared that, as a Chinese, he did not find it extraordinary.

"It is typical of thousands of our intellectuals today," he said. "Kwei Chu was broken by love. His own personal emotions were the most important thing in life to him. Of course! The intellectuals have nothing else. Even the revolution, to most of them, is nothing but an emotion; not a life and death necessity as it is for the masses. I am surprised that Kwei Chu did not try to kill himself—but he did not have enough courage even for that!"

Chinese Destinies: Sketches of Present-Day China, pp. 146-58. See the editors' introduction for a general discussion of the 1920s, including the Northern Expedition (1925-27), the phenomenon of Chinese seeking a foreign education as a kind of status symbol, and the White Terror of 1927.

Yes, he was right. I recalled the suicides in Manchuria and North China—boys and girls who preferred death to renunciation of love. In Mukden one day, a girl rather than be forced by her parents into marriage with a man she had never seen, plunged into the river. The week following, in Peking, a man student took his life for a similar reason. Almost daily young men or women have killed themselves over their thwarted or endangered love. Too weak to defy their old feudal families openly, too unclear to leave and declare war on their choking restrictions, they seek an end of their suffering in death.

Kwei Chu was different from these. He did not kill himself. He is broken.

It began like this. When Kwei was eighteen his father arranged his marriage with a village girl. He had been brought up in Honan, educated by private tutors and in an old-fashioned small town school, and he had never heard of a son refusing to marry when his parents wished it. Nor had little Lian Shiang, the girl chosen for him. They had played together as very young children, and both took it for granted that when a girl married she went to live in the home of her husband's parents, where she served them almost as a slave. If happiness came to help her bear her burden of duty it was by accident but not by right.

Kwei and little Lian Shiang had been married three months when Kwei's father sent him away to Tokyo to study. He thought a business education would enable his son to become a bigger and better merchant than he himself had been. For, despite his long nose that everybody said meant riches for a man and that had been the chief inducement when his wife's parents chose him as a son-in-law, he had not become rich. Even after twenty years, he had only a small shop connected with his house in the village and a part-interest in a town shop. His frequent trips to town gave him grand ideas;

and he came to desire a cunning, sharp-witted son, trained in new-fangled ways, to build up his town business. He himself harbored the desire to buy a certain sing-song girl as a concubine. If he became rich he could have more than one, all of them very young. So he sent Kwei to Tokyo to help him achieve these noble ends.

But Kwei was much like his gentle little mother and had no wish to learn business; he went to Tokyo with a heavy heart. Little Lian Shiang's heart was heavier still. Since their marriage she had taken her place in his family and had worked harder than she had ever dreamed any daughter-in-law ever worked.

She had the daily harrowing criticism, nagging and quarreling of a number of elder people to endure—aunts, grandmother, grandfather—the demands of younger children to meet. And since her new parents were old-fashioned she served them constantly. Even when they ate she could not sit, but had to stand until they had finished. When Kwei's father came home late at night after a gay party with his men friends and with gay women in a certain house in the town, little Lian Shiang arose from her bed, prepared food for him, and stood silently while he ate. There were times at night when she lay close to Kwei and wept in exhaustion. And one day Kwei thought he could endure it no longer.

He found his father in the shop filling boxes with little cakes. The old man would fill the bottom with small, bad, ugly cakes and then cover them all with a nice layer of big round fresh ones. The peasants were simple and honest folk and they would not know the difference until they got home. The old man paused in this honorable pursuit to listen to his son's request for a conversation. Kwei began in a respectful manner, saying that Lian Shiang was becoming thin and ill from overwork, insufficient food and bad treatment. He asked that this cease. His father's only answer was to turn angrily and leave the shop without a word. That his son should appeal for his own wife filled him with disgust.

For these reasons Kwei often found difficulty in studying in Tokyo. His wife once wrote him a few awkward characters, and sometimes she could steal away and pay a professional letter-writer a few coppers to write for her. Her letters kept before his eyes the monotonous suffering of her life, and often bitterness filled his soul. For he had a tender affection for her. Once he wrote his father a sharp letter of protest. But after that he heard no more from her, and only one curt note from his father telling him to be ashamed for trying to give advice to his own parents!

When Kwei sought comfort from his student friends, he learned only that most of them had even greater troubles. His room-mate, Li, was also from Honan. Although Li was only twenty-four years old he was the father of four children. And his wife was an ignorant, foot-bound woman, of no will, no ideas, no ambition whatever. Like a dumb animal she merely waited for his instructions. His other friends told of the same troubles: old-fashioned wives who thought their chief duty was to "bear sons," to serve their husbands and parents-in-law without will. His friends spent long hours discussing or reading of new ideas abroad in the world. And it was through them that he first studied the revolutionary movement in his own country.

The knowledge of his own country came upon him like a mighty flood. For it was the year the revolutionary army was marching from Canton north-ward, leaving the flower of China's youth upon the battlefields behind it but awakening tens of millions of China's masses.

The Chinese revolution found its strong, clear echo in the ranks of Japanese workers and revolutionary students. There for the first time "dangerous thoughts" were expressed, and to his astonishment Kwei began to realize dimly that the revolution in his own country meant more to these Japanese than it did to himself or many of his well-to-do Chinese countrymen.

Masses of demonstrating workers swung through the streets of Tokyo by the thousands, carrying great banners: "Long live the Chinese Revolution! Victory to the Chinese Revolution! Victory to the World Revolution!" He saw Japanese police attack these marchers, beat, arrest, imprison them. In the university Japanese students were arrested—picked off here and there to disappear from the eyes of man. There were mass meetings in public places and Kwei would rush to the place, only to be grabbed by policemen, searched, and ordered to leave unless he wished to be arrested. Unclear, uncertain, he would leave.

At other meetings he was smuggled through the police cordon and listened to Japanese workers, Koreans and one or two of his own countrymen uttering words of fire. Sometimes it seemed the Japanese speakers were jealous of the Chinese revolution. Once he heard a speaker declare: "Here we are, a highly industrialized society, yet our Chinese comrades with a feudal agrarian background are ahead of us! The shame of it, comrades!"

Kwei talked to many of his countrymen who were students in Tokyo. The rich ones hated these Japanese workers and revolutionary students. They were dangerous Communists, they said. Dangerous—to whom?—percolated through Kwei's brain, but slowly and dimly. Without knowledge, without the driving force of necessity, he was whipped back and forth from one idea to another.

But these new ideas took on less importance still in his mind after he saw the Japanese girl in the house next door to that in which he and his friend Li lived. This came about through the Japanese violin he had bought

when he first came to Tokyo. For although his father
envisaged in his son a cunning and able business man,
Kwei showed little aptitude for such a profession. He
had bought a violin and paid more attention to it than
to a serious study of how to make money. One day
from the adjoining house he heard another violin. He
paused in his playing to listen. The violin from beyond
the wall paused also, as if the player were listening. He
played; it played! Such a thing as this seemed more
interesting than the whole Chinese revolution. Daily he
watched the house next door. From Li he learned of a
girl student who lived there with her family.

Then one day he saw her! She stood on the veranda,
not far from him, a small, slender girl with fair skin and
long, black eyes, and a heavy braid of black hair down
her back. The wind came down the street bending the
birch trees before it, and it caught in her long kimono
sleeves and lifted them like the wings of a bird. The
kimono was green and the lining brilliant red; there was
a small brilliant red patch at the throat. Kwei watched
what he thought the loveliest sight he had ever seen.

The little girl on the veranda saw him watching her.
Shyly she returned his gaze, and she must have seen the
gentleness in his face, for she did not run away. She was
even braver and more modern than he, for she spoke:
"You play the violin beautifully," she said, smiling.
Kwei's heart stood still and he could only gaze at her in
rapture.

There were always ways to meet the girl after that.
There were well-planned accidental meetings on the
street; or he would suddenly discover her sitting on a
bench in the near-by park. He turned from study and
from thoughts of the Chinese revolution to working up
ways of meeting her. He found that her name was Kico
San and that she would soon graduate from a high
school. Her parents had learned of her meeting him and
viewed the acquaintanceship with growing dislike. For

Kwei was a Chinese, and the Japanese of this class considered the Chinese an inferior people. Kico San did not—no, no, she was a modern girl.

Kwei would listen to her low, sweet voice that effaced from his mind all thoughts of anything but her. She was gentle and obedient as are almost all the women of her country; still she disobeyed her parents by meeting him secretly. And he dressed as a Japanese student when he went to meet her, that the police might not interfere as they often do when a Japanese girl is seen with a Chinese.

Kwei did not at first tell Kico San that he was married. As the wonderful months passed he himself almost forgot it. But when he realized that he was coming to love her with a love such as he had never had for little Lian Shiang, he recalled his marriage vividly. It was clear to him that Kico San loved him also, for he had tested her. Sometimes he had worn his Chinese clothing and they had walked together in the park; and when a policeman stopped them to ask who Kwei was the girl had angrily rebuked him. Nor did she even see the disapproving stares of people who passed.

Kwei had tested her in other ways also; he took her to meetings of her own countrymen where she listened with growing interest and approval to "dangerous thoughts." She went with him so willingly, so unquestioningly, and threw her heart so much into what she had heard, that Kwei began involuntarily to think of the two of them going through life like that. They would return to China together where there was a revolution—but then he remembered Lian Shiang, working like a slave for his parents, longing for his protection.

One late afternoon when there were no lectures Kwei met Kico San in their accustomed place in the park. When he saw her face turned toward him, his decision to tell her of Lian Shiang almost vanished. But he forced himself to speak. When he had finished, the two of them stood in silence for a long time. Then Kico San bowed gently, turned and went away without a word.

After that the weeks passed and there were no more accidental meetings. He lay awake through the nights; he prowled through the parks where they had once met; his violin brought no reply from the house next door; his life became like a barren desert. The revolution in his own land might come and go; he lived only within the realm of his own personal misery, helpless and hopeless.

Then fate stepped in and at first seemed to solve the dilemma for him, almost as if some one had written a drama about his life. A telegram from his father called him home. His mother was said to be ill. And since he was without personal will, he did as told.

When he reached home, his mother herself met him at the door. From her he learned for the first time that it was little Lian Shiang who had been not only sick, but who had died. She had died four months before and her grave was already green. He had not even been informed and his father had now called him home only for his second marriage—for the family needed a daughter-in-law to do the work Lian Shiang had done. The shock was very great for Kwei, for he recalled the months he had passed with Kico San while his little wife was being worked to death by his harsh, primitive father.

But Kwei had learned at least something in Tokyo, and his new ideas he took seriously, even tragically. Especially if they had to do with his own person. So, finally facing his father, he blurted out things no son in China says to a father. The misery of life seemed to be wrapping itself around him, and the man before him seemed responsible. At last he burst out: "I will not give you another wife to work to death!"

Hardly had the words left his mouth when his father struck him full in the face, then grasped a stick and struck him viciously over the head.

When Kwei came to consciousness, the sad, tear-stained face of his gentle mother was bending over him. He lay for one month after that and recovered with great difficulty. When he was able to walk again he asked his father, formally, to be good enough to permit him to return to Tokyo. As a reply his father took a handkerchief from a shelf in the shop, unfolded it, and showed Kwei a little pile of letters. Kwei saw the feminine hand in Japanese characters, and he knew from whom they had come. All had been opened, and the boy knew his father had called some friend in the city to his aid in reading them. Kwei reached out to take them, but his father turned and threw them in the brazier, lit them, and stood over them until they had burned, together with all their precious secrets. The boy watched, white-faced. Then his father informed him that he must either marry or never be permitted to study again; and that in no case would he be permitted to return to Tokyo.

It was a month before Kwei worked out his plans and finally journeyed to the little near-by town. Then he went to two merchants who were friends of his father. These men all knew him as a boy who had had an escapade, but still as an honest lad. When he came to get money which he said his father needed, they gave it to him and he signed for it. That night, with three hundred Chinese dollars in cash and no baggage but the clothing on his back, he left in a third-class railway carriage en route to Tokyo.

When he arrived at last, he learned from Li that Kico San's family had moved away suddenly, leaving no address. They had arranged a marriage for their daughter, but she had caused a scandal by refusing. Someone had told Li that the family had gone to Yase, their native village.

That same afternoon Kwei took the train for Yase, and for days he searched for Kico San. Disappointed, he returned to Tokyo and began a search that lasted for weeks. First he went to the police; then to the school where Kico San had studied. The only trace he found was from a student girl who told him that Kico San had learned of his wife's death from Li. She had written to him when her parents tried to force her to marry. But he had not even replied, and at last she had become ill and was removed to a hospital.

Kwei found the hospital. A nurse told him that Kico San had indeed been there for a number of weeks, suffering from a nervous breakdown. She had wept much and shocked her parents and the physicians, but interested the nurses, by calling out his name and coupling it with the most intimate of words exchanged only between lovers. "Oh, my Life! Oh, my Life!" she had cried. But the nurse did not know where the family had now moved. She asked Kwei to remain and talk, for here was a chance for rare gossip. But he turned, blinded with disappointment, and went away.

For weeks after that Kwei searched for Kico San. He walked through the streets, watching every girl that passed, searching side-streets, hoping against hope. The whole city seemed leagued against him, a Chinese, trying to find the Japanese girl he loved. Often he would see a small figure in a distance, the wind catching in the long sleeves of her kimono. He would hurry until he reached her side, only to turn away in despair.

Hope gradually dried up in his heart, like water in a spring. And one day he went into a wine shop and drank. After that he drank more and more, blindly, desperately, filled with hatred against himself and every one else, and often he lay deadened with wine by the side of the road, conscious only of the rickshas and automobiles rushing past. He spent days and nights in a drunken stupor, dirty and unwashed, and his money slid through his fingers like sand. The world of men with all their standards became as nothing to him, a youth of a race called inferior. And Kico San became a symbol of life's purpose that had vanished.

Kwei became a notorious drunkard. When he was sober his friends would argue. Some were ashamed that he should love beyond control, and above all a Japanese girl, when every one knew the Japanese despised the Chinese. Others told him of the fate of the revolution in China, of the counter-revolution that had begun. Was it not his duty to stop all his personal stupidities now that revolutionaries were being butchered, they asked? Was it not his duty to attend the great mass meetings of Japanese workers and students and protest against the White Terror?

Kwei listened silently to all the good advice. Through his blurred brain filtered a bit of pride that he was causing such a sensation among his friends and countrymen. They were all talking about him! He had never been disciplined in thought or action, and now he let his personal emotions have full reign—straight to destruction. Once Li and two other friends took him rowing on a lake outside the city and there began giving him good advice again. He suddenly arose and, without a word, violently hurled himself overboard. One of the men dived in after him, but he fought for the right to die, and only when some one stunned him by a blow on the head with an oar could they get him to shore alive.

It was shortly after this that the Japanese army invaded Shantung and bombarded the city of Tsinan-fu. Kwei was sober when he heard the news and listened to his friends discuss a protest meeting they were calling. Through Kwei's mind swept all his bitter hatred against the Japanese who had robbed him of Kico San. Now these same Japanese had bombarded a Chinese city. Something stronger than his love for Kico San took possession of him, and from that moment he never drank again. It was as if he had been sick for a long time and had suddenly begun to recover.

When the mass meeting was held Kwei was in the very midst of it. Japanese police stood about the hall and even on the platform. Yet one by one the speakers came forward: first the Chinese who had formed the "Big Alliance" of all groups of their countrymen; then Japanese who thought "dangerous thoughts." Then a Korean spoke, two policemen standing on either side of him; but he spoke, keeping his tense face to the audience, knowing as did all present that he and the other speakers would be followed to their homes, perhaps beaten into unconsciousness on the streets, then arrested and imprisoned.

The meeting was finished and the audience was leaving the building peacefully when the police attacked. Under their merciless clubs men and women fled in every direction, and the wounded lay bleeding on the streets. Two friends saw Kwei, with a gash down his cheek and his clothing torn in shreds, trying to lift himself from the pavement. Crouching as they ran, they grabbed him by the shoulders and dragged him as they would a sack of grain, down streets and under the trees into a park. Then, after a long silent watching, they carried him to a wine-shop.

"He's been drinking?" the owner asked. The friends nodded assent, and the three of them washed the blood from his face and brought him to consciousness.

The following week they argued with him to leave Japan. "Come home with me," one student urged. "I would rather never study than study in such a country as this!" So Kwei left Tokyo with his friend. They were followed nearly to Peking by a Japanese spy who showed an all-embracing interest in them.

And there in Peking Kwei lives today, a frail, gentle, broken youth, but still with a kind of unyielding, stubborn manliness about him. His clothing is the one suit on his back, his socks are the legs of his underwear drawn down long and folded over his toes; his bed is three boards nailed together and covered with a padded quilt. His food is millet porridge and some salted vegetables. The appalling poverty in which he lives is shared by his student friends. They hardly know what recreation means, and money for car-fare is a luxury. Magazines or books of "dangerous thoughts" circulate from hand to hand amongst them. Such thoughts are not a pleasant dabbling in new ideas that tickle the fancy; they are a desperate and grim necessity. Most of them know fully what such ideas mean, know fully the price they must pay if they are discovered.

Often Kwei talks with his friends. Many of them are hard and clear-minded and know the way they must travel. But Kwei does not. He bends forward, his arms resting on his knees, and talks out the things that press on his young heart.

"Sometimes I do not sleep," he says. "My way is so narrow, so closed in. I see no way out. I have no money to study and I am trained to do nothing. Thousands of men of training and experience are without work. . . . I could get help from my father if I agreed to marry the girl he has chosen for me, but why should I obey him? I hate this man called my father. . . . Our families are a great load dragging all of us youth down to the bottom of the sea. I know so many young men ruined in this way. You may say we deserve it, or we would rebel. . . . In my native village they do not even know how to rebel; it is not we who are to blame—it is the system."

"Then help us destroy this system!" some one angrily interrupts him.

Kwei regards his frail, girlish hands, as if studying their possibilities.

"How?" he asks senselessly. "I see no way out. . . . My way is closed in. And now something is wrong with my mind. . . . I cannot remember things very well. . . . Those things shocked me and drove me mad and now I do not see any way out. But all I know is I shall never

marry.... I must find some way to work only for
China."

"For China! For China!" some one else interrupts.
"Which China do you mean—the masses or the rulers?
The people or their butchers? You are still a futile
intellectual—helpless, hopeless! Our way is very
clear—very clear! For there is only one way; you know
what that is—you know we dare not speak out the
words. Show me any other way! You have already
traveled that other way—into the swamp of your own
emotions. Why continue?"

Kwei answers listlessly: "Yes, you are right. You are
always right. But still—" his voice trails off into
nothingness. And his friends turn to their work and
leave him contemplating the emptiness of his own
existence.

Sometimes Japanese women pass Kwei on the streets.
He always watches them intently, as if still searching. Of
one Japanese girl who passed, a friend remarked to
Kwei: "She is very beautiful." As if drawing upon the
wells of a deep conviction, Kwei replied. "No! She is
not beautiful—that is dead beauty! Nor is her kimono
beautiful. Sometimes, beneath, they wear green
kimonos—with red in the sleeves and a red patch at the
throat. The wind catches the sleeves and lifts them like
the wings of a bird."

THE MARTYR'S WIDOW

As Deng Yin-chu sat in prison in Nanking awaiting death, he reviewed the troubled, harassed years he had spent with his wife. Her one visit had revived memories. They were not pleasant ones. But now she had paid the prison director one hundred dollars for the privilege of talking with him for a few minutes, and she had told him that she had raised thirty thousand dollars to save him. With this money she had arranged with the prison director and judges to manage his escape. He had glowed with joy and sat waiting for the consummation of her promise.

Deng felt conscience-stricken when he recalled his treatment of Hwa-chuan in the past. Yet there had been reason enough for his actions. For years he had struggled with her. The revolution had pulled him in one

Chinese Destinies: Sketches of Present-Day China, pp. 237-53.
Sun Ch'uan-fang was a local warlord.

rection, she in the other. A wife of his family's choice,
he had still learned to love her. This love had remained
unbroken until 1925, one year before his arrest. Their
three children had bound her more closely to him. He
had never understood her even though he had loved her.
She spent most of her time gossiping at tea and mah-
jong parties, decorating herself with new gowns, and
caring for her complexion. But this was perhaps the way
of women.

Also, she loved money, but perhaps this was not so
bad, for he himself had no conception of its value, and
during the ten years of his marriage he had turned his
entire salary over to her. This money she had deposited
in a Shanghai bank in her own name and through an
agent had loaned it out at such usurious rates of interest
that she had nearly doubled it. With the eyes of a greedy
gambler she had watched it grow. But Deng had excused
her, saying this was only to guard the family from hardships. He felt certain now that it was this money she was
using to save his life.

He recalled how he had tried to interest her in public
affairs. First he had bought books and magazines for her
to read and with enthusiasm had tried to impart some of
his thoughts and knowledge to her. But his books and
magazines she hid in a box in the store-room where they
mildewed and rotted. And when he tried to impart his
ideas to her, she turned to him a fretful and resentful
face.

"What business is it of yours who rules China?" she
complained. "You have a good position and you are
earning a good salary. If you get mixed up in these
dangerous plots, it will only endanger me and our children."

Of the men friends who came to see him she had first
been suspicious, and when she heard them talking of the
same things Deng had tried to impart to her, she became

so hostile that gradually she drove them one by one from his home.

Deng sought in her a friend and comrade, as well as a wife. From his friends and their teeming thoughts and their secret plans he would repeatedly return to try to convince Hwa-chuan. His friends, wiser, repeatedly warned him to keep his affairs from her, but he loved her and it was not easy. As the revolutionary movement spread his conflicts with her grew, and only when the tears rolled down her face would he repent. With her in his arms he would finally sink into their bed, and, smothered by her caresses, he would promise to protect her, to sever himself from all friends or activities that endangered her. For a time she would rest content, their life would be peaceful, and then he would be drawn back to his own thoughts and plans. The conflict at home would be renewed; again it would end by his wife's weeping in his arms in bed; and he, mastered by her body, would give her new promises.

Sometimes he had awakened at night to think of this harassing struggle. His friends were right, his wife wrong. Yet he did not have the strength to follow his convictions. Then his mind would travel back to the first woman who had mastered him. This woman had been his father's concubine and his father had paid many thousands of dollars for her. Nearly ten years his senior, it was this concubine who taught him the secrets of what is called love.

He had been a youth of seventeen at the time. For four years after that he had secretly waited to do her bidding, as a tailless dog awaits the command of its master. Watching her with jealous eyes, he had grown into a morose, silent young man laden with sickly passion and guilt. Then his father, as if sensing something at last, suddenly sent him abroad to continue his studies. Even when, a short time afterwards, he learned that the

concubine had sickened and mysteriously died, her power over him was not broken. He sought her in every
woman he met. And when he agreed to the wife his
family chose for him, he dreamed of her only as the first
woman in another form.

Deng recalled how he had often sat up in bed at night
and gazed into the dim face of his sleeping wife, seeking
in her some resemblance to the other woman. There was
none. She was short of stature, fair of skin, and with
small eyes. Hers was a dead, stupid beauty, like the face
of a doll. She worked hard to preserve a certain pretti-
ness. But the first woman had been tall and slender,
with long black eyes that could burn with passion when
he held her to him. Her body had been like a slender
bamboo swaying in the breeze, responding to every
breath of his desire. He could recall nothing she had ever
said—but then women are supposed to have nothing to
say. She was the beginning and the end of his expecta-
tion from woman. Yet there was something in his wife
that recalled this woman. When he held her in amorous
embrace, his memory of the past revived and he lay
again in the arms of the concubine. For these precious
memories he had for years slighted his friends and the
revolution.

Deng recalled the night he finally freed himself from
his wife, the night a new passion took the place of his
old memories. It was on the evening of May 30, 1925,
when the news of the Shanghai massacre flashed
through all China. All work had ceased and everywhere
men stood talking of strikes, boycotts, fighting. That
evening he had returned late, expecting to find his wife
as excited and determined as was he. She met him, smiling prettily. She had heard nothing of the news. And
when he told her of it, she looked vacantly into his face.

"These people are always doing something bad," she
said fretfully. "They are always trying to stir up trouble!"

"What do you mean?" he asked, confused and astounded.

"Down there in Shanghai—the workingmen and students. They have no sense of responsibility. Your friends are the same—they are a bad influence upon you."

His arms hung lifelessly at his sides and he stood staring into her empty face.

"Now what have I done?" she began, her lips quivering, tears gathering in her eyes. She placed her hands on him, clung to him. But he continued staring at her as if she were a strange woman. Then he firmly and slowly released her arms, and without a word or a backward glance turned and left the house.

From this time he had worked in secret, always silent in her presence. Her fretfulness, her resentment, and her tears crystallized into a hard, mean hatred for his friends and the movement that was sweeping China. She peddled her grief from one tea-table to the other in Nanking, and her gossip reached the ears of Deng's friends. Deng merely replied to them: "She knows nothing of our work. I never speak to her of it." But they worried, for her tongue wagged.

Finally an impetuous man by the name of Wu decided to act. One day he appeared in her home and spoke directly: "I hear what you are saying about Deng's political activities. I warn you—you are endangering his life. If your gossip reaches the ears of the militarists he will be arrested and killed."

She was white with fury. "You are all Reds! It is you who are endangering his life. What right have you to force him into these activities. He is *my* husband!"

"I have warned you, seriously. The militarists have ears at every keyhole. Nobody complains of him but you."

"You are a bad man—leave my house at once!" she screamed.

Hwa-chuan peddled her new injury over the city. Wu, the Red, had insulted her! When Wu heard her new attack, he quietly packed up and moved, fearing his own days would be few. And when Deng raised his firm voice in protest at her conduct, she had screamed in fury at him and run from the room.

Then had come Deng's arrest and within a few hours his sentence to death charged with high treason. Hwa-chuan was stricken not so much by grief as by resentment and anger. When his friends called and asked her, as his wife, to go to the prison and negotiate with the authorities about bribery, she had first accused them of every crime. They waited only for her to finish. Then, in straight, hard words, they asked her to recall that even were all she said true, still the problem now was to free her husband. This she could do, but none of his friends would dare risk their lives by negotiating for him.

"And who will pay this bribery?" she furiously asked.

"We will," they assured her.

Her fury slackened as they spoke of the money. And at last she agreed.

Hwa-chuan passed in and out of many doors in Nanking, and finally thirty thousand dollars was fixed upon as the sum that would make Deng's escape from prison possible. It was a huge figure, for Deng's friends were poor. Hwa-chuan had more than this in the Shanghai bank but not a breath of it passed her lips. It was Deng's friends who had got him into this trouble, it was *they* who should pay for it! Then the money began to pour into her lap. First Deng's old father wired fifteen thousand dollars from Szechuan and prepared to leave for Nanking to help his son. Deng's friends collected money in driblets—one thousand here, five thousand there.

Finally the entire sum lay in Hwa-chuan's hands. She gazed at it and thought what a shame it was to give so much money to the authorities. Hwa-chuan felt her power, and money also meant power. She began bargaining with the judges and jailers, just as she bargained with shop-keepers.

"Thirty thousand is too much—we are poor . . . we do not have so much money . . . I will give you five thousand . . . seven thousand then."

Then as the days and threats heaped themselves one on the other she offered ten thousand. The execution was twice announced and twice postponed as the authorities waited for the money. But they demanded the full thirty thousand. More, they were insulted that she tried to make them lose face by bargaining with them just as if they were common men of the street instead of high and powerful officials.

Friends, with perspiration standing out on their foreheads, haunted Hwa-chuan's house. Pay the full thirty thousand, they pleaded. Pay it! Hwa-chuan smiled when she saw their dependence on her, these men who had treated her so badly but a week before!

"If I free Yin-chu," she said, "will you promise to leave him alone and not draw him into your traitorous activities in the future?" The men looked at her with black eyes filled with some emotion that might have been fear or hatred.

"Yes, we promise," they answered. "We promise you anything—only pay the money and free him."

"I will pay," she said, "but these authorities will take less if we hold out a little longer. I know how to deal with them."

The situation was altogether a most interesting and exciting one for Hwa-chuan—just like some of the novels she had read. She often pictured herself in the rôle of a heroine in a novel—one of the great beauties who held the destiny of empires in the palm of their fair hand. She recalled how by cunning and sex charm women of the past had raised their own families to eminent positions and destroyed their enemies. She recalled a more modern novel in which a traitor had been shot. The traitor's friends rescued his body and found it had only one bullet wound, and it not fatal. They had brought the man to consciousness and nursed him back to health. In fantasy Hwa-chuan saw herself doing the same thing. She would charm the authorities—thereby saving ten to fifteen thousand dollars—she would smash the friends of Deng who were responsible for his imprisonment, and if in the end her husband was shot, she would bring his body in a motor car to a hospital and nurse him back to life.

Hwa-chuan set about the realization of her dreams. Returning from the prison one day after fruitless bargaining and tea drinking, she felt she should adopt new tactics. She went to a silk shop and bought a number of new gowns, then drove by ricksha to her tailor's and gave instructions for their immediate preparation. She would appear in ravishing new gowns before the authorities. But, emerging from the tailor shop, she could not endure the thought of returning home to face the perspiring men who haunted her house day and night, urging, pleading, promising. Her life was hard enough without hearing their voices each day! Upon her shoulders rested the whole burden of saving Deng's life and of saving half the money! Harassed by these difficulties, she drove to a fruit-store and selected a basket of choice mangoes. With these she went to the home of a friend, where she spent the weary hours of the afternoon eating mangoes and relating her sorrows and problems.

The next morning Hwa-chuan arose languidly to confront her difficulties again. But, outside, the city was astir with the report that on this day Deng Yin-chu was to be shot. Some one sent Hwa-chuan a note informing her of this, but she took it lightly, shrugging her shoulders and thinking, "This is the third threat. They are merely trying squeeze the thirty thousand dollars out of me!"

Within an hour the streets of Nanking were lined with people. Others streamed from every direction. Foreigners mingled with the crowds of the curious. Down the streets came marching a long line of soldiers—and in their midst, his hands tied behind his back, the tall, slender figure of Deng Yin-chu. He was without a hat, and his thin, sensitive face was pale and desperate. To the gaping thousands that did not lift a finger to save him from the soldiers, he cried:

"I am being taken to execution! I am a member of the Kuomintang! I have worked for the revolution! Down with Sun Chuan-fang! Down with all the oppressors of the people!"

The crowds stared, now and then a man snorting a short laugh. Thousands fell in behind the procession, pressing close to the marching soldiers, struggling to see just how a man acts on his way to death. At the place chosen for the execution, the dense mass of people formed a semi-circle. With the same expectant excitement that they would watch an old feudal play, they now watched the soldiers line up and await the moment of firing. Men fought to get in a front row that they might see better.

Deng Yin-chu was marched to a cleared space before the soldiers. Standing alone before the firing squad, but facing tens upon tens of thousands of men and women who stood and gaped, he raised his head and cried into the spiritual desert of China:

"Down with Sun Chuan-fang! Down with the oppressors of the people! Long live the rev . . . !"

A volley of shots cut his last word short. His body trembled, then crumpled together and sank to the earth, his face burrowing a small groove in the dust. Another volley of shots buried themselves in the prostrate form. Then an officer strode forward, kicked the body over until it lay face upward, lifted his pistol and buried a shot right through the mouth of the dead man.

In the crowd a man fell to the earth, unconscious. The crowd gave way to his falling body, then stood staring down at him stupidly, laughing a bit. Nobody bent even to touch him. Some one reached out and kicked him in the side with his foot to see if he was dead. The body did not move. A small circle stared down at him for a few seconds, then turned to the greater drama again. . . .

The soldiers were marching away, the body of Deng Yin-chu left to be devoured by dogs. It was forbidden to remove it, for Deng was a revolutionary. The crowd moved forward, stared its fill at the body, then began to seep away into the city to relate the drama to their friends and families.

Finally there remained but a small group of the insatiably curious, also one prostrate body of an unconscious man, and one man who stood as if petrified, staring into the void. At last the man of stone came to life and began to walk away. His eyes fell upon the prostrate figure. With a gasp he knelt down, turned it over, and cried, "Wu . . . Wu!" The unconscious man returned to the earth again, the man of stone cried for rickshas, lifted the limp figure, and drove away with it.

Among those who turned and dashed from the crowd of gaping thousands was Hwa-chuan, Deng's wife. When the news had finally reached her that Deng was being marched through the streets to execution, she had telephoned a garage for a motor car. In her mind was the story in which a man was shot, rescued by his friends, and nursed back to health. She would rescue her husband in the same dramatic manner! But when she reached the execution grounds she could not break through the dense crowd. She had heard not one shot, but a whole volley. There had followed the second, as if a whole army was in action. Then a final pistol shot. A man, perched on the shoulders of another, said: "Well, there's not much left of *that* fellow!" Confused, astounded, Hwa-chuan had turned and rushed home in her motor car. When the chauffeur demanded a forty cent tip, she shouted at him, "You've got wind in the head!" and left him sitting with his hand outstretched.

That night through a rain storm that drenched Nanking a number of dark figures crept through the darkness over the place where Deng's body lay. They halted, whispered, heaved something up, and crept onward. Where Deng's body had lain outstretched was a long dry spot that soon blended with the surrounding mud. The next day the press reported that the body of the traitor had been stolen in the night. The dogs of Nanking had been robbed of a feast.

Deng's father arrived two days afterwards. He remained for a week. At the end of that time he returned to Hwa-chuan's house, packed up his bundle, and then, with a face that looked like that of a corpse, said to her: "It is you who have killed my son!"

Hwa-chuan began to cry. "It is not my fault! It is Wu and Tsai and Wang and their crowd who have done this. They led Yin-chu astray. I tried to save him.... I worked like a slave! It is easy for them to accuse me now. I am only a woman and a widow. I am defenseless, with three little children! If Yin-chu were alive, they would not dare attack me like this!"

The old father waited for her to cease raving. Then once more he said: "You have killed my son! You would not even pay the fifteen thousand dollars I sent to save him!"

Her eyes red from weeping, the woman bitterly sobbed: "I suppose you even want that money back now.... You would even take it from Yin-chu's children!"

The old man turned and with slow, dragging steps left her house.

Hwa-chuan was left alone. Deng's friends who had formerly haunted her house seemed to have been swallowed up in a void. To the women friends who came to console her—and there were few—she wept out her grief. It was those Red friends of Deng who had killed her husband! She named them repeatedly. And when her accusations reached their ears, one by one they packed up their belongings and disappeared from Nanking.

In the great historical events of the period the details of Deng's killing were forgotten. His name, the name of a Kuomintang martyr, remained. And gradually Hwachuan became known as the widow of a martyr, the mother of a martyr's sons.

The revolution rolled and seethed, the southern army captured Nanking, the old militarist army fled. The year 1927 rolled on; the revolution broke on the cliffs of the class struggle; and in the place of the old, the new militarists established their own government in Nanking. The Kuomintang was purified of everyone but the militarists, the landlords, and their intellectual apologists. Many of Deng's friends led the lives of hunted animals.

The new militarists claimed Deng as one of their martyrs, and upon his widow and children they settled life pensions. To his widow they gave large sums for his funeral and for a memorial. And when she murmured that the pensions were enough only for ordinary living, they gave her additional sums that his children might later be sent abroad for university education.

Hwa-chuan, the widow, became known as the true and faithful wife of a revolutionary, as a woman who had stood like a rock by the side of her husband aiding him in all his work. She herself often recalled the trials of secret revolutionary work of the past. Officials called upon her, she was showered with presents and attention. She was asked to honor the government with her presence—"to continue Deng's work where he had left it."

With her new official duties, it was impossible for the widow of a martyr to be burdened with Deng's children. She wrote Deng's old father in Szechuan and suggested that he take his grandchildren and rear them. For now she was only a widow, it was hard for her to support herself and her children on her meager salary. After all, she wrote, the children belonged to the Deng family. So one day a member of the family appeared in Nanking and took the three children back with him to Szechuan.

Hwa-chuan was now free to "continue Deng's work where he had left it." In preparation for this difficult task she went to Shanghai and bought a number of new gowns and a good store of foreign perfume, cold cream, powder and rouge. She had her hair permanently waved. With these aides she was able to remove all trace of her former sorrows and difficulties.

So completely did she succeed in her duties that the eyes of an old official fell admiringly upon her. He had formerly been an official in Hunan and was an old Kuomintang member. He, by name Fu Kwang-chuang, was so rich that Hwa-chuan's heart almost ceased beating when she thought of him. A henchman of the new militarists, he had been one of those who had helped "purify" the province of Hunan when the counter-revolution began. The press reported at the time that "he had put his thumb down on the Reds in his own district—and it was a heavy thumb."

Hwa-chuan demurely returned Fu Kwang-chuang's admiring gaze. True, he was married to an old-fashioned woman whom he had left on his estate in Hunan; and true, he had ten children. But in these revolutionary days divorce is not difficult for an official.

A short time afterwards the chauffeur in the employ of Fu Kwang-chuang told the porter in Fu's department some news. The porter told another friend, and the friend told a lower official. Sometimes, he said, the old boss called on Hwa-chuan in the evening and left only the next morning! This news went the rounds and in time reached the ears of Hwa-chuan herself. One day she called to interview the powerful and honorable Fu, and as she passed down the corridor the brushes of many of the clerks came to a standstill. She turned resentfully as some one laughed. At the end of the month two men on whom her unfortunate eyes had fallen were informed by their chief that their work was so bad that they would have to find employment elsewhere. The guilty chauffeur lost his job and the porter found himself on the street.

Then came the incident at Shanghai. The head of one of the sub-bureaus in Fu Kwang-chuang's offices went to Shanghai over one week-end to take in the latest movies, dance halls, and visit the sing-song houses. One night when he returned to his hotel he came face to face with the old official and Hwa-chuan. They were just entering a room, and when they heard steps they had turned. He was so astonished that he had halted and stared. Returning to Nanking on the following Monday, he was at once called to the office of his powerful chief. The old man made a little speech about the principles of their late master, Sun Yat-sen, and expressed his appreciation of the young man's devotion to duty. Such devotion should not go unrewarded under the new revolutionary régime. The young man was promoted to be head of one of the chief bureaus in the department. For continued devotion to duty further advance would be equally rewarded.

The young official expressed his deep gratitude and assured his chief that he was willing to give his life for the revolution and for the party to which they both belonged. His chief could depend upon him in all emergencies.

Next, the accountant for the department began to have considerable trouble. The expenses were mounting with each month. Shanghai firms from which the department bought supplies were sending blanket accounts, and sometimes false ones. Here were two of the latest bills he was asked to pay. One was itemized and included twelve ladies' handkerchiefs at three dollars each. The second included two tablecloths with napkins, a bolt of silk and a box of silk stockings.

The old official looked in surprise at the accounts. There was some mistake! He would investigate. A few days later the accountant was called in and given two new bills. The one for the handkerchiefs was changed to a dozen hand-towels for the department, and the second one was a blanket account marked miscellaneous. At the same time Fu Kwang-chuang arose and delivered a little speech. He was delighted to have under him an accountant who kept his eyes open and looked after the expenditure of the department. This honesty was rare in officials these days, as Chiang Kai-shek had said in his recent speech. Henceforth the accountant's salary would be increased forty dollars a month, and further devotion to duty would meet with like reward!

The accountant expressed his appreciation for the raise and said that although he was not working for money and found it highly humiliating to have to accept any salary at all for his service to the party, still with famine, floods and Communist depredations in the interior, he was forced to depend upon money for his existence. In the future, as in the past, he would continue his unselfish labors!

Hwa-chuan, one of the choicest flowers of the Kuomintang, "continued the work that Deng had left unfinished" in many ways. There was the time she came face to face on a public street with Wu, the former friend of Deng who had warned her that her gossip would yet lead to his death, the same Wu who had fallen unconscious when Deng had been shot. He was now dressed in a disgraceful old foreign suit and hat, and across his upper lip was a scar as if some one had smashed him in the mouth. Elegantly gowned, a picture of Shanghai art, she had still halted and smiled charmingly at him. But instead of returning her smile, he greeted her ironically by her maiden name, saying:

"I hear you are a great revolutionary now, Sun Hwa-chuan!"

She looked at him suspiciously and then resentfully. "I am doing my duty!" she replied.

"As in the past!" he remarked.

Hwa-chuan's resentment turned into anger. "I have heard that you, as in the past, are still a Red! Still working against the government!"

Wu smiled. Furiously, to show her knowledge and power, Hwa-chuan continued: "In fact I have seen your name on the list of men the government intends to execute!"

"Perhaps you will help them, Sun Hwa-chuan—as in the past!" Wu replied. Then he scornfully walked past her and made his way down a narrow street.

That evening Hwa-chuan wept. Fu Kwang-chuang could not endure to see tears in the eyes of his little treasure. It was all because of the insult of this man Wu whom she had met on the street, she told him. Wu Chung-hwa was a Red and was one of those who had caused Deng's arrest. Now he insulted her in the streets!

The old man became furious. Before another night had passed the man should be in the hands of the police! But his little treasure should not weep her eyes out because of such a bandit. She should have those jade earrings she had so much admired, and she should have anything else she wanted.

The tears continued rolling down her face: "It is only because I am a poor woman, and alone, that people can treat me like this," she gulped. "If Deng Yin-chu were alive, he would protect me. . . . But to you also I am only a widow to play with. Your old wife has the protection of your name and position—I have nothing!''

Fu Kwang-chuang protested. He loved her. But his wife was old, the mother of his ten children. It would look bad if he took a young wife.

"Yes," she wept, "I am but the widow of a martyr! I am good enough to give my life for the revolution but not good enough for you to marry!"

The old man sought to kiss her tears away. And at last he lay trembling in her arms, smothered by her caresses, promising to do anything she wished.

At another time Hwa-chuan complained to him: "Everybody is gossiping about us. But I know who is responsible. It is Professor Wen Fu-an. He tries to deny that he is a Red, but Deng Yin-chu told me in secret that he was. This is the reason he is creating a scandal against us!"

A few days later a friend called to warn Wen Fu-an that he should leave Nanking at once or face arrest as a Communist. Wen was astonished. He was not a Communist at all, he said. That did not matter, the friend declared, considering the source of the rumor. When Wen heard the name of Fu Kwang-chuang, he recalled the death of Deng Yin-chu at the hands of the old militarists. The old militarists killed by the dozens, the new militarists by the thousands. That night he took the night train for Shanghai.

Finally the day came when Hwa-chuan's long years of suffering for the revolution came to an end. Fu Kwang-chuan divorced his old wife and settled a part of his fortune upon her and a part upon his children. Upon Hwa-chuan he settled a large sum of money and some of his Shanghai real estate. This he had done before he and she were married, for, weeping in his arms, she had expressed the fear that unless she had the property in her own name, his children might one day challenge her

right to any of his fortune. She did not wish to suggest
that he would die before she did—she would rather die
than think of such a possibility! But in case he *did*, it
was best to be prepared.

Following the divorce and the settlement Hwa-chuan
walked to the table where a modern marriage ceremony
was gone through, the old man proudly at her side,
claiming as his own the revolutionary widow of a
revolutionary martyr. There were many speeches about
the benefits of modern marriage, marriage based upon
love, and about the birth of a new society as expressed
in such unions as this. "In this marriage," one speaker
poetically cried, "we have love presiding over the
revolution. Could anything be more hopeful for the
future of China?"

One of the speakers was the young official from the
old man's offices. This man had taken up a collection
from all the employees of Fu Kwang-chuan and had
bought a present of great value. Representing his
colleagues, he delivered an oration on old Fu's
self-abnegation in official life. As he spoke tears sprang
to the eyes of many a guest and even the old man
himself cried.

After the wedding Hwa-chuan spoke with deep
feeling to friends who congratulated her: "Now I feel
that I can be of more service than ever to the
revolution!"

REFU-
GEES

Approaching Hankow
January 8, 1938

We changed trains at Chengchow on the Lunghai railway
last night. As we approached that city we saw many
slogans on the various station platforms. A large one
read, "Myriads of men with one heart fighting to the
very last." The region swarmed with troops, though this
is true of all North and North-west China. It seems that
three-fourths of the entire population is in uniform.

On the station platform at Chengchow were many
refugees. They had their entire worldly possessions on
wheelbarrows—including pitchforks and rice bowls. A
few were men, but most were women and children. In
the semi-darkness they sat or stood, many of them

*China Fights Back: An American Woman with the Eighth Route
Army* (New York: The Vanguard Press, 1938), pp. 279-84. This
is an excerpt from Smedley's diary, dated January 8, 1938, near
Hankow in central China.

absolutely still. I saw two men standing as still as statues. About them were their long white quilts. They reminded me of American Indians. At their feet, and about the platform in all directions, were huddled women and little children, their quilts wrapped about them. But many had no quilts at all.

We talked with the refugees. They are all peasants from a town in Western Hopei—the very region where the Eighth Route Army and the Partisans are fighting the Japanese columns moving against them. We held a memorable conversation with a thin, straight old woman who had no coat and no quilt. Her wrinkled skin was like parchment and her voice was hoarse and harsh.

"There is fighting between the Partisans and the Japanese in West Hopei?"

"Right!" she answered in a voice as cold as a frozen river.

"There is great suffering there?"

"Right! Great suffering!" She was grim and all other words seemed superfluous and superficial.

"How old are you?"

"Seventy-two."

"How did you come from West Hopei?"

"Walked—since late November."

In her words, her voice, her motionless figure, was an indescribable grimness. At the age of seventy-two she was a wanderer on the frozen roads of the North. Suffering had stripped all things from her, even words.

We halted before a woman enveloped in a quilt. From beneath the quilt, at her bosom, the voice of a tiny child wailed. On the outskirts of the quilt sat huddled a little child no more than two years old. I bent down and put her under the quilt, then drew the covering about her. The little thing lifted her face and smiled at us, smiled as an adult would smile, gratefully. The face was sweet and tender. Half-frozen, not a sound of complaint came from her.

"We have had nothing but hot water to-day," one of the refugee peasant women said to us. "We have not eaten at all. Give us money."

I had just six dollars, and it was doubtful if our military pass would be accepted on the express to Hankow. If we had to pay, six dollars was not enough. I would have to borrow from one of my companions who had a bit more than I. So I could not give money. Six dollars—for a few hundred people! It was hardly a drop in a bucket. And so, feeling like a miser, I kept my six dollars and explained to the refugees why I had nothing to give.

To enter a third class railway carriage in China these days required careful planning.

"Let's plan our campaign," one of our party began. "When the train comes in, we will hoist Wang Shih-fu on our shoulders and put him through a window. Then we can hand him the baggage. Then you help me in through the window, and *you* go through the doors at the end of the carriage."

The train came in, the windows high above our heads. Both ends of every car were packed with fighting, struggling masses of human beings. To join that fighting mass was to risk injury. So we hoisted our men on our shoulders and thrust them through the windows and in the end I waited to enter through the doors at the end of the car. The inside of the car was like a battlefield, filled with three or four times as many people as there were seats. The aisle was clogged with them, with bundles, big and little baskets, boxes and suitcases. Everyone walked up and down the little mountains of bedding, and the owners did not care. The baggage racks that ran the length of the car were piled with baggage— and with men stretched along on top of the baggage.

Through this mass came a rich landlord's family, their way being cleared by soldiers. This family, consisting of five or six women and six or eight children, parked

themselves right across from us. The landlord was like a
Turkish Sultan with his harem. Soldiers brought in the
family's luggage. And it consisted of everything imagin-
able. Other luggage on the racks was shoved away or
thrown off in the aisle and dozens of pieces of
household goods, bedding, clothing, baskets, bundles,
suitcases, took their place. The aisle for a third of the
car was piled high with the family luggage. And after
having filled every available space, the landlord directed
the soldiers to put other pieces in between the seats in
which passengers sat. Without any "by your leave" they
began piling bundles right in on my feet. Where we were
to put our feet was none of their business.

I arose, lifted the bundles being piled on me, and
hurled them over into the aisle and on the feet of the
ladies of the seraglio. Consternation unheard of! But the
family was like an avalanche that had merely met a
slight impediment. So they diverted the flow to other
passengers—who fatalistically accepted it as they would
accept a Yellow River flood.

When the war is over and the poor peasants and
soldiers have defeated the Japanese, he probably will go
trundling back and expect to get his land back—and
expect the peasants to pay him a half or two-thirds of
the rent.

Sleep was impossible on the straight, narrow, board
seats, and the air in the car was unbearable at times. So I
watched and listened to other passengers. Behind the
high seats in front of us some soldiers were talking. One
was a petty officer. Their problem was the withdrawal
of the Chinese Government from Hankow to Szechuan.
How should this be done, and so on and so on.

My guard remarked, "They are talking only of
retreating. They are too pessimistic. Why talk of retreat
and not of advance?"

Behind me I heard a group talking tenderly and I
arose and looked back to see a father holding up a baby

in his arms and talking to it. The child was just learning to talk, and the father was teaching him his first words:

"Down with the Japanese!" the father said.

The tiny voice of the child repeated, "Down with the Japanese!"

"Down with the traitors!"

"Down with the traitors!" piped the little voice.

Down the aisle was another family scene, but a cruel one. A mother constantly bawled at her three- or four-year-old child. The woman's voice resounded through the whole car. She had a white, cold, cruel face and once I saw her hit the little child three or four times right across the face. The attack was so fierce that a man across the aisle arose and reached over and rescued the child. The cruel mother followed, beating the head of the child, and when the strange man's arm protected it, she beat the arm. The child was sobbing bitterly.

This was the first cruel Chinese mother I have ever seen. Chinese mothers are generally very tender, and even spoil their children. So I wondered if this woman were not half insane, or if, instead, the child perhaps belonged to the former wife of her husband.

In another little compartment back of us a Chinese woman began preaching Christianity to those about her. She was threatening mankind with the coming end of the world. This war was a sign of it. When this didn't impress anyone, she threatened them with death and with hell fire after death. That didn't seem to interest anyone either. So she told them that the foreigners do not want China to become Christian, that they do everything to prevent the Chinese people from knowing the truth of Christianity. At this I saw a man smile, then yawn, huddle up in his corner, and go to sleep. And so the woman's wisdom fell upon the desert air, and she soon ceased talking.

The Chinese people are tough customers when it comes to religion. The only way most of them can be caught is to get them during a flood or famine and then give rice to those who accept "the one and only true faith." This woman had tried to catch them by the war, but she didn't offer anyone any rice. And, after all, people with money enough to travel third class are not yet at the end of their rope.

We arrived at Hankow at midnight to-night, and ricksha coolies pulled us through the streets for two hours and a half, to earn more money. They knew we were strangers and did not know the way. After an interminable time we reached the local office of the Eighth Route Army. It is in the Japanese Concession, which has been taken over by the Chinese. We went to an empty room, spread our sleeping bags and quilts on the floor, and slept.

CHI- NESE PA- TRI- CIANS

In China, as in classic Greece, "family women" never associated with men as friends or comrades. Only a few girl students dared become actresses, though many were learning to walk openly in the streets with men friends. In China, as in Greece, no man of education did physical labor. Theirs was the realm of intellect and they lost face by physical work.

In feminine fashion I challenged the Peking patricians on the score of the backwardness of the wives of respectable men, on the concubine system, and on courtesans. Some asserted that courtesans were at least better than the prostitute system of the West. Worse, I insisted, for the West recognized prostitution as an evil; in China men's desires were absolute. A Chinese woman who dared take a lover could be "set aside" by her husband and family; the man never.

They spoke of the old family system in which the possession of concubines gave a man "face." The

Battle Hymn of China (New York: Alfred A. Knopf, 1943), pp. 50-57.

concubines were bought and could be sold or given away to subordinates. A poet who became my friend even asserted that concubines were the only opportunity for love that a man had. "Ridiculous!" I protested. "The concubine does not choose love—she is bought."

This poet had broken with the family system; like many other men he had refused the wife chosen by his family although she had been taken into his father's home as daughter-in-law. He himself had followed the modern way and married an actress; his family had not recognized the marriage and had refused to receive the new wife. Once he told me he could love no woman over twenty who was not beautiful, did not have a willowy waist, or weighed more than a hundred pounds. Often when he and I sat in the tea-houses, the restaurants, or the old Peking theater I would ask him to select from the women around us those he considered beautiful.

"You choose empty, baby-faced women," I told him.

He was always sorry that I was a woman and that he could not smuggle me into an evening party at the home of some wealthy *hetaera*, mistress of one of his patrician friends. He himself had no courtesan mistress, but now and then let his gaze fall upon the wife of some other man.

Some modern men married educated women, but soon the family system devoured the wives. The wife ceased to keep abreast of her husband intellectually. While he sought love outside the home, she became merely the mother of his children. When I asked such a wife what she read, she answered: "Oh, you see, I graduated ten years ago and shortly afterwards married."

A few strong-minded modern women kept pace intellectually with their husbands. They were feminists of will and decision. Woe to the husband of such a woman if he tried to take a concubine or crept to a courtesan! When I listened to these women I wondered if the old custom of foot-binding had not been simply a clever device to cripple women and keep them submissive.

For a time I was a companion of the patricians; and with a few I remained good friends. To them I was not man, woman, concubine, or courtesan. I was a foreigner who was no longer young, was not beautiful, earned her own living, and associated with men as an equal. Neither wifehood nor love was my profession.

Most of the patricians were humanists. Some, influenced by John Dewey, were pragmatists. Many, too, had been affected by Bertrand Russell's superlatively keen analyses of society and his crystal-clear atheism. They agreed with him, as I did, that if there had been no fear of death, there would have been no belief in immortality. (But they opposed his book on China because it praised China's evils and made the young people arrogant.)

In their pragmatism these patricians tended to distrust any movements that had not proved practicable. They approved American democracy, but questioned Russian Communism. I argued that the Soviet Union no less than America had had to chart a new course in history and, like Revolutionary America, was fighting for it against European opposition; but they asserted that Marxism was still only an experiment in the Soviet Union and had not proved itself. Many Chinese students believed in it, and some peasants and workers in southern China were fighting for it, but they themselves opposed it. Some insisted that there were no classes in China and that this idea had merely been invented by Marxists. One told me he thought the Chinese Communists should be given a province in which to experiment;

if it proved practicable, other provinces might copy it. Science and education were the way to progress, they said; look what science had done in the West. I argued, of course, that Communists also used science and education.

One patrician, an interesting and thoughtful man, was an anthropologist who spent much time excavating ancient Chinese settlements in the valley of "China's Sorrow," the Yellow River; buildings, utensils, works of art, oracle bones, and even cowrie shells, a form of money fashioned like the female genital organ—perhaps a relic of some ancient matriarchal system—were unearthed. This was valuable and precious, I admitted, but what about the present? The region in which they worked was the scene of wars, Yellow River floods, and famine. Millions of peasants had repeatedly been driven from their homes. For a bowl of noodles or rice they had sold their land to war-lords, landowners, or officials. Even their most essential possessions—primitive agricultural implements—had to be bartered in the market. Their sons poured into the armies to earn their rice; their wives and children were sold as servants, and their daughters as prostitutes or concubines. Driven by hunger, these peasants had stripped the land of all shrubs and trees, selling them as fuel in order that they themselves might eat. When the rains came, no plant was left to hold the water in the soil. "China's Sorrow" overflowed and desolated the land. Then had come the wind storms. The top soil had been whirled away in great clouds, and the desert had crept ever nearer. In some Chinese cities, one could walk on sand dunes that rose to the top of the city walls. Soon, I said, they too would become buried cities of the past.

"Why unearth dead cities now?" I asked. "Excavate them fifty years hence when the conditions that make more dead cities have been wiped out!"

Of course, that meant taking part in politics, and of course politics was corrupt and dangerous. Even if the patricians entered politics, they would merely be swallowed up, I was told. They must wait for better days, they said. But I wondered who could afford to wait.

In Peking I visited a match factory. All but the foremen and a few men manning the engine were little children who had been bought from the peasants. Long lines of them, some hardly more than babies, stood twelve hours a day before trays filled with matches, their small hands working like lightning as they filled match-boxes. A foreman carrying a short stick walked back and forth along the aisles.

Each day the children were fed two meals of millet gruel and salt; sometimes there were a few bits of greens and sometimes a little lard. To keep warm they slept crowded close together on long *k'angs*, earthen platforms extending the length of barrack-like rooms and weakly heated by a coiling flue beneath. I asked about one child, covered by a thin quilt, lying on a *k'ang*. He had been sick for three days; no one knew why and there was no medical care. He would either live or die.

In China death moved about as bold as a lord. It found a home in the grisly poverty of peasant huts. It came in the form of tuberculosis or heart failure to miners and factory workers. It haunted the dreams of the rich, who armed themselves with foreign machine-guns to meet the threat of peasant rebellions such as had overthrown dynasty after dynasty. Foreigners living luxuriously in the port cities feared it in every advance made by China, whether through the nationalist Kuo-mintang or through a peasant revolution led by Communists.

Death walked arm in arm with poor students, but they braved it and thought only in terms of the social revolution. So I said to the patricians: "Your philoso-

phy of death is false! The students do not accept it. Else
why are they rebellious, searching the whole world for
the way to a better life?"

In these degenerate days, argued the patricians,
students were undisciplined and irresponsible, using
school and university dormitories merely as centers of
propaganda. How true this was I do not know. Certainly
some students had become revolutionaries overnight.
Was this not because they had no way of putting into
practice what they learned? Forbidden by tradition to
do physical labor, they were frail, delicate, almost a race
apart. Despite this, many students, studying intensely,
became critical and bitter, challenging death and intimi-
dated neither by prowling spies nor by policemen's
clubs.

Some patricians gave me a dinner one night, and I
began to understand why many foreigners loved Peking,
cultivated Chinese friends, and studied the language. We
started for a restaurant that had in other days entertained nobility. Leaving the compound of the old
Chinese house where I lived, I pulled the red-lacquered
door behind me just as a coolie was passing. My fur coat
seemed to awaken some childhood memory in him.
With his face turned toward the wintry sky he broke
into a lullaby about a tiger with a fierce fur skin but a
tender heart beneath. Until he reached the corner he
sang to a cold snowy world; then, surely, as did the
whole leisure-loving Peking populace, he halted in a
crowd to laugh at a clown or juggler, a dancing bear, or
perhaps some big swordsmen from Shantung performing
in the streets.

My friends joined me. As we entered the old Chinese
restaurant, waiters bawled until the open rafters trembled: "Eight guests arrived!"

Sing-song girls were wailing, apparently running
scales—and taking in all the flats as they passed—to the
accompaniment of a screeching Chinese violin. The

songs were from some Peking opera. The singing mingled with the raised voices of men playing the finger drinking game—in which the loser must each time drain his cup dry. Their voices mingled with those of waiters bawling announcements of new guests. The noise must have warmed the heart of the restaurant-owner, for he kept smiling and bowing.

Several waiters brought open charcoal braziers to our room and others appeared with many small cups of various wines, one of them the cool, white, treacherous *bei-gar*. After my hosts had sampled the liquors, they gave their orders, and soon small pitchers of cold *bei-gar* and hot wine were brought in, along with platters of *hsiao chirh*—literally "small eats." Then came the manager, ever bowing and smiling, and behind him a column of waiters with the famous Peking ducks, ready plucked, which we had seen hanging from the rafters as we entered. Our hosts felt the various ducks like connoisseurs, selected the best, and sent them away to be braised.

Meanwhile we sat about drinking from our ever full wine-cups, eating, laying down our chopsticks politely, and conversing. One short fat guest lifted his cup and cried: "Bottoms up!" That reminded him of a friend who had not quite mastered English, but wished to show off before some foreign guests. He had lifted his winecup and solemnly announced: "We will now show our bottoms!"

Once after a gale of laughter had subsided, one of my hosts exclaimed: "I repeat: There are no classes in China. Classes! Marxians invented the idea! My ricksha coolie and I can laugh and talk like old friends as he pulls me through the streets."

"Would you be his friend if you had to pull him through the street?" I interrupted. "Or if he revolted? You are friends only so long as he accepts his inferior position."

"*I also* am a proletarian. I work for my living," replied my table companion complacently.

One of my hosts lifted a heap of fried chicken livers on his chopsticks and placed them on my small plate. The poet who later on became my friend called for paper, brush and ink and began to create a Chinese name for me. I objected to such a name as Beautiful Plum Blossom or Lotus Bud or Perfumed Brook. Finally he gave me the old Chinese family name of "Shih" and added the two syllables "mei ling." When I rejected the latter, he merely Latinized the name to "Shih Mei Di Li," which had no meaning at all; but because it had four syllables he called me a Mongol. My christening called for more wine and for a poem about the waves of the sea. I seemed to have responded with a song. It must have been "The Streets of Laredo," for that is the one song I really know. It was hailed as a work of classical art.

Then the duck! First we all sat and looked at it admiringly, assuring each other that it was a thing to see, then die. Our hosts shook their heads deprecatingly, calling it most inferior. With a slight clatter we leveled our chopsticks on the table, then all plunged in together, lifting bits of the thin-sliced skin and flesh onto the fine pieces of unleavened pancake before us. We tapped them elegantly with a mixture of sauces, laid a baby onion on top, rolled the pancake up, and took a bite. We closed our eyes prayerfully for a second, then looked at our hosts gratefully, like beggars. The dams of sound split wide open after that. We drank and ate, pausing only to argue amiably about Chinese women and patricians and proletarians. The courses kept coming and the wine flowed.

When at last we rose to depart, a waiter went into the courtyard and bawled out the size of our tip, and as we went down the courtyard another waiter took up the cry. A third echoed it as we passed out. We were like an army of generals parading between columns of saluting privates. This gave us tremendous "face" and encouraged other guests to give generously. What a difference it makes if a waiter bawls out a tip of two dollars rather than ten cents!

We rode home in rickshas through the cold white streets, and someone behind me began to run scales in high falsetto about a prisoner who refused to be rescued because the prison was the prison of love. I took an oath that I would never, never leave Peking, but would become a patrician myself even if it took all my life. This oath became mixed up with thoughts about my ricksha coolie silently running like a tired horse before me, his heaving breath interrupted by a rotten cough. Suddenly his broad shoulders began to remind me of my father's. I was a dog and the whole lot of us were dogs!

"Listen, you!" I screamed at my hosts in most unpatrician tones. "Get out and pull your ricksha coolie home! Let's all get out and pull our ricksha coolies home! Let's prove there are no classes in China!"

MADAME CHIANG KAI-SHEK AND HSIAO HUNG

Madame Chiang Kai-shek came to town for treatment of an old back injury and I met her for the first time in the home of one of her sisters, Madame H.H. Kung. A few foreigners had once tried to arrange a meeting between Madame Chiang and myself, but I had been unwilling to run the gantlet which her followers had arranged for my benefit. Once her devotees were out of the way, I met her and found her cultivated, tremendously clever, and possessed of charm and exquisite taste. She was

Battle Hymn of China, pp. 523-24. The scene is Hong Kong in 1940-41. Bishop Hall was Bishop Ronald O. Hall, a liberal-minded cleric at whose home in the country (Shatin) Smedley recuperated for a few months. Hsiao Hung and her husband, Hsiao Chun (Tien Chun), were refugees from Manchuria who became close associates of Lu Hsun. Both were talented writers. In the 1940s and 1950s Hsiao Chun emerged as a major novelist. His *Village in August* was the first modern Chinese novel to be translated and published in the United States (New York: Smith and Durrell, 1942).

groomed as only wealthy Chinese women can be groomed, with an elegant simplicity which, I suspect, must require a pile of money to sustain. Next to her I felt a little like one of Thurber's melancholy hounds. She was articulate, integrated, confident. As the years had made her other sister, Madame Sun Yat-sen, older and sadder, so had they increased Madame Chiang's assurance and power.

Emily Hahn, living in Hong Kong, had just finished her book on the three Soong sisters. They well deserved a book, but contrary to the belief of some foreigners, they were not the only capable women of China, and I always considered it unfortunate that publicity should be given to them alone. I often wondered what would have happened to the whole Soong family if they had been born in the obscurity and poverty that bound most of the Chinese doing duty in the war zones. I thought of those Chinese women who were doctors, nurses, political organizers and educators in the armies and among the people, and who, despite the indescribable hardships under which they worked, kept growing in power and ability with the years. And I thought too of those others who lost the bloom of youth in the struggle, and died at obscure posts.

A new Chinese womanhood, in many ways far in advance of American womanhood, was being forged on the fierce anvil of war. One such woman lived with me for a time in Bishop Hall's country home. Her name was Hsiao Hung and her fate was typical. When the first Japanese attack on Manchuria had begun in 1931, she had fled. She had fled not only from the Japanese, but also from rich parents who wished to marry her off to a husband of their choosing. She had kept just ahead of the Japanese advance, living first in Peking, and then successively in Shanghai, Hankow and Chungking. Her first book, *Fields of Life and Death*, had been introduced to the Chinese public by no other than Lu Hsün, and he had spoken of it as one of the most powerful modern novels written by a Chinese woman. After this the girl published three other books, including a war novel which she completed while living in my home. Like most modern Chinese writers, she lived in perpetual penury. The money such writers earned placed them on the economic level of the coolie class. So Hsiao Hung, like many of her colleagues, contracted tuberculosis. I had her admitted to the Queen Mary Hospital and kept her supplied with money until Hong Kong fell. She died a few days after the Japanese occupied the island. She was twenty-eight years old.

The Japanese had learned enough in China to develop some political cunning, and they began applying it soon after their first days of orgy in Hong Kong. They began posing as men who were liberating the Chinese from white imperialism. Thus when Hsiao Hung's husband [1] asked for permission to cremate her body and take the ashes to Shanghai to be buried beside her "master," Lu Hsün, the Japanese granted the request. So clever were Japanese tactics in some respects and so emasculating had been the influence of British policy on the Hong Kong Chinese that many Chinese chose to live under Japanese rule in Hong Kong rather than go into China.

[1] Her husband, Tien Chun, was author of the well-known book *Village in August.*

SILK WORK- ERS

Just as I arrived in Canton in the hot summer months of 1930, another General was killed by his bodyguard for the sake of the fifty Chinese dollars offered by a rival General. Such events had begun to strike me as sardonic. The Kwangtung Provincial Government was semi-independent, but in the hands of generals who took by violence what they considered their share in the loot of the south. They whirled around the city in bullet-proof cars with armed bodyguards standing on the running boards. Such was the spirit of the generals and of the officials whom they brought to power with them.

Battle Hymn of China, pp. 86-92. For an earlier, more abbreviated version of this story, see *Chinese Destinies*, pp. 116-19. Smedley's accuracy and insightfulness have been confirmed by recent scholarly work on the subject: (see Marjorie Topley, "Marriage Resistance in Rural Kwangtung," in *Women in Chinese Society* eds. Margery Wolf and Roxane Witke, [Stanford: Stanford University Press, 1975], pp. 67-88).

I interviewed them all and put no stock in what they said. They treated me magnificently, for foreign journalists seldom or never went south in the hot summer months. So I had a Government launch to myself, with an official guide to show me factories, paved roads, new waterworks and the Sun Yat-sen Memorial Hall. For truth I depended on Chinese university professors, an occasional newspaper reporter or editor, teachers and writers, the German Consul in Canton—and on my own eyes and ears.

The real reason I went south in the hottest part of the year was to study the lot of the millions of "silk peasants" in a silk industry which was rapidly losing its American markets to Japanese magnates. But I did not wish to see the silk regions as a guest of the powerful Canton Silk Guild, for the Guild, after all, was like a big laughing Buddha, naked to the waist, his fat belly hanging over his pajama belt. At last I found a group of Lingnan Christian University professors who were engaged in research in the industry. One young expert was leaving for the Shuntek silk region for a six weeks' inspection tour. I went with him to the Canton Silk Guild, where he argued with a suspicious Guild official until given permission to travel on Guild river steamers and enter the region in which millions of peasants toiled. There the millionaires of the South Seas had erected many large filatures; the spinners were all young women.

Next day the young expert and I boarded a river steamer. Some twenty or thirty Guild merchants were the only other passengers. The steamers had armor plating and machine-guns to protect the merchants from "bandits." The "bandits," I learned, were peasants who took to the highway for a part of each year in order to earn a living.

I once calculated that, if these "bandits" had attacked and captured our steamer, they would have secured enough food to feed a whole village for months. At meal times the merchants hunched over the tables, eating gargantuan meals and dropping the chicken bones on the floor. They talked of silk, money, markets, and of how much their firms were losing. The silk industry was indeed fighting for its life, but if there were losses, it clearly did not come out of the hides of these men. I pined a little for Jesse James.

My young escort was awed by these men, but when he spoke of the silk peasants or the girl filature workers, hostility and contempt crept into his voice. His particular hatred seemed to be the thousands of women spinners, and only with difficulty could I learn why. He told me that the women were notorious throughout China as Lesbians. They refused to marry, and if their families forced them, they merely bribed their husbands with a part of their wages and induced them to take concubines. The most such a married girl would do was bear one son; then she would return to the factory, refusing to live with her husband any longer. The Government had just issued a decree forbidding women to escape from marriage by bribery, but the women ignored it.

"They're too rich—that's the root of the trouble!" my young escort explained. "They earn as much as eleven dollars a month, and become proud and contemptuous." He added that on this money they also supported parents, brothers and sisters, and grandparents. "They squander their money!" he cried. "I have never gone to a picture theater without seeing groups of them sitting together, holding hands."

Until 1927, when they were forbidden, there had been Communist cells and trade unions in the filatures, he charged, and now these despicable girls evaded the law by forming secret "Sister Societies." They had even dared strike for shorter hours and higher wages. Now and then two or three girls would commit suicide together because their families were forcing them to marry.

For weeks my escort and I went by foot or small boat from village to village, from market town to market town. The fierce sun beat down upon us until our clothing clung to our bodies like a surgeon's glove and the perspiration wilted our hat bands and our shoes. At night we took rooms in village inns or pitched our camp beds under mosquito nets in family temples. All the roads and paths were lined with half-naked peasants bending low under huge baskets of cocoons swung from the ends of bamboo poles. Market towns reeked with the cocoons and hanks of raw silk piled up to the rafters in the warehouses. Every village was a mass of trays on which the silkworms fed, tended night and day by gaunt careworn peasants who went about naked to the waist.

At first curiously, then with interest, my escort began to translate for me as I questioned the peasants on their life and work. Their homes were bare huts with earthen floors, and the bed was a board covered by an old mat and surrounded by a cotton cloth, once white, which served as a mosquito net. There was usually a small clay stove with a cooking utensil or two, a narrow bench, and sometimes an ancient, scarred table. For millions this was home. A few owned several mulberry trees—for wealth was reckoned in trees. But almost all had sold their cocoon crops in advance in order to get money or food. If the crop failed, they were the losers. Wherever we traveled the story was the same: the silk peasants were held in pawn by the merchants and were never free from debt.

Only as we neared big market towns, in which silk filatures belched forth the stench of cocoons, did we come upon better homes and fewer careworn faces. The daughters of such families were spinners. It was then that I began to see what industrialism, bad as it had seemed elsewhere, meant to the working girls. These were the only places in the whole country where the birth of a baby girl was an occasion for joy, for here girls were the main support of their families. Consciousness of their worth was reflected in their dignified independent bearing. I began to understand the charges that they were Lesbians. They could not but compare the dignity of their positions with the low position of married women. Their independence seemed a personal affront to officialdom.

The hatred of my escort for these girls became more marked when we visited the filatures. Long lines of them, clad in glossy black jackets and trousers, sat before boiling vats of cocoons, their parboiled fingers twinkling among the spinning filaments. Sometimes a remark passed along their lines set a whole mill laughing. The face of my escort would grow livid.

"They call me a running dog of the capitalists, and you a foreign devil of an imperialist! They are laughing at your clothing and your hair and eyes!" he explained.

One evening the two of us sat at the entrance of an old family temple in the empty stone halls of which we had pitched our netted camp cots. On the other side of the canal rose the high walls of a filature, which soon began pouring forth black-clad girl workers, each with her tin dinner pail. All wore wooden sandals which were fastened by a single leather strap across the toes and which clattered as they walked. Their glossy black hair was combed back and hung in a heavy braid to the waist. At the nape of the neck the braid was caught in red yarn, making a band two or three inches wide—a lovely spash of color.

As they streamed in long lines over the bridge arching the canal and past the temple entrance, I felt I had never seen more handsome women.

I urged my young escort to interpret for me, but he refused, saying he did not understand their dialect. He was so irritated that he rose and walked toward the town. When he was gone, I went down the steps. A group of girls gathered around me and stared. I offered them some of my malt candy. There was a flash of white teeth and exclamations in a sharp staccato dialect. They took the candy, began chewing, then examined my clothing and stared at my hair and eyes. I did the same with them and soon we were laughing at each other.

Two of them linked their arms in mine and began pulling me down the flagstone street. Others followed, chattering happily. We entered the home of one girl and were welcomed by her father and mother and two big-eyed little brothers. Behind them the small room was already filled with other girls and curious neighbors. A candle burned in the center of a square table surrounded by crowded benches. I was seated in the place of honor and served the conventional cup of tea.

Then a strange conversation began. Even had I known the most perfect Mandarin, I could not have understood these girls, for their speech was different from that spoken in any other part of the country. I had studied Chinese spasmodically—in Manchuria, in Peking, in Shanghai—but each time, before I had more than begun, I had had to move on to new fields, and all that I had previously learned became almost useless. Shanghai had its own dialect, and what I had learned there aroused laughter in Peking and was utterly useless in the south. Only missionaries and consular officials could afford to spend a year in the Peking Language School. Journalists had to be here, there, and everywhere.

I therefore talked with the filature girls in signs and gestures. Did I have any children, they asked, pointing to the children. No? Not married either? They seemed interested and surprised. In explanation I unclamped my fountain pen, took a notebook from my pocket, tried to make a show of thinking, looked them over critically, and began to write. There was great excitement.

A man standing near the door asked me something in Mandarin and I was able to understand him. I was an American, a reporter, he told the crowded room. Yes, I was an intellectual—but was once a worker. When he interpreted this, they seemed to find it very hard to believe.

Girls crowded the benches and others stood banked behind them. Using my few words of Mandarin and many gestures, I learned that some of them earned eight or nine dollars a month, a few eleven. They worked ten hours a day—not eight, as my escort had said. Once they had worked fourteen.

My language broke down, so I supplemented it with crude pictures in my notebook. How did they win the ten-hour day? I drew a sketch of a filature with a big fat man standing on top laughing, then a second picture of the same with the fat man weeping because a row of girls stood holding hands all around the mill. They chattered over these drawings, then a girl shouted two words and all of them began to demonstrate a strike. They crossed their arms, as though refusing to work, while some rested their elbows on the table and lowered their heads, as though refusing to move. They laughed, began to link hands, and drew me into this circle. We all stood holding hands in an unbroken line, laughing. Yes, that was how they got the ten-hour day!

As we stood there, one girl suddenly began to sing in a high sweet voice. Just as suddenly she halted. The whole room chanted an answer. Again and again she sang a question and they replied, while I stood, excited, made desperate by the fact that I could not understand.

The strange song ended and they began to demand something of me. They wanted a song! The *Marseillaise* came to mind, and I sang it. They shouted for more and

I tried the *Internationale*, watching carefully for any reaction. They did not recognize it at all. So, I thought, it isn't true that these girls had Communist cells!

A slight commotion spread through the room, and I saw that a man stood in the doorway holding a flute in his hand. He put it to his lips and it began to murmur softly. Then the sound soared and the high sweet voice of the girl singer followed. She paused. The flute soared higher and a man's voice joined it. He was telling some tale, and when he paused, the girl's voice answered. It was surely some ballad, some ancient song of the people, for it had in it the universal quality of folk-music.

In this way I spent an evening with people whose tongue I could not speak, and when I returned to my temple, many went with me, one lighting our way with a swinging lantern. I passed through the silent stone courtyards to my room and my bed. And throughout the night the village watchman beat his brass gong, crying the hours. His gong sounded first from a distance, passed the temple wall, and receded again, saying to the world that all was well.

I lay thinking of ancient things . . . of the common humanity, the goodness and unity of the common people of all lands.

YOUTH AND WOMEN'S COMMIT- TEES

One afternoon and evening the Youth and Women's Committees gathered in a woman's conference with delegates from many parts of the province. I was the chief speaker, and because I was foreign I was expected to give an extensive report on the international women's movement. It was the most difficult lecture I had undertaken, for I had only fragmentary information on the subject. I did my best, but I knew that I was learning much more about the women of the interior of China than they were learning about foreign women. The room was packed with women, including many who were soon to have babies. Most of them were educated, but a number were peasants and workers. They had decorated the hall with banners carrying such slogans as *Unite all anti-Fascist forces of China with the women of the world*! and even one that hailed me as the *Mother of Chinese Wounded Soldiers*!

Battle Hymn of China, pp. 353-54. The setting is central China in 1939.

A group of war orphans, dressed in tiny military uniforms, had gathered wild flowers from the hills and presented them to me along with eloquent little messages to American children about the determination of Chinese children to struggle until China was free. The women refugees in the spinning and weaving factory had sent me two pairs of white cotton stockings, and the women of the Youth Committee had written a poem of welcome in which they declared that they had been trampled under men's feet for thousands of years, but foresaw a new dawn.

From these women I learned once again of the fearful handicaps under which Chinese women labored. Many said they would never marry until China was victorious, for family life imposed such burdens that married women could seldom take part in public affairs. This was a rare thing to hear, for marriage is considered the duty of every Chinese girl, and if they reject it the pressure put upon them by their families makes life a misery. Women beyond the age of twenty-five were considered "old," and after that age few thought they would ever have an opportunity to marry.

They told me that the masses of women were illiterate, untrained, without disciplined habits of thought, and still bound by feudal customs. In some villages in Anhwei there were still "baby-ponds" in which unwanted girl infants were drowned at birth. Girls were still affianced at a very early age, sent to their mothers-in-law to grow to maturity, and then married. The cruelty of mothers-in-law to "child brides" was a problem so universal that the Women's Committee often had to rescue little girls and keep them in their headquarters.

The secretary of the Women's Committee, Miss Chu Ching-hsia, an educated married woman in her middle twenties, once said to me:

"The Ta Pieh mountain range was once a soviet region in which women unbound their feet, cut their hair short, studied, and took part in public life. But now they have let their hair grow; women with short hair had been called Communists and killed by the Kuomintang armies. When we first went to them as organizers, we proposed that women cut their hair and take part in anti-Japanese organizations. They were afraid lest the Terror begin again.

"It is very strange. Most of these Chinese soviet women cannot read or write, yet they know all about capitalism and world affairs, and they speak very well before meetings. When we convinced them that they would not be killed if they took part in public life, they and the men of the villages were able to manage the local anti-Japanese associations without any help from us.

"We educated women find women's work very difficult. Our lives, habits, and standards of culture are so different from those of the country women that it is difficult to find contacts with them. So we have now brought a group of country women here for training.

"We have another strange problem. The soviets forbade forced marriages; men and women were allowed to marry from choice and neither side could pay a dowry. The Kuomintang called this 'free love.' But now, when the soviets no longer exist, some men lay claim to the women to whom they were affianced in childhood according to the old custom. Sometimes these women are stolen or taken by force from their homes. They may be widows whose husbands were killed in the civil wars or are now fighting in the Eighth Route or New Fourth Armies. But the childhood engagement is considered legally binding, and our Women's Committee is always having trouble forcing the men to return the stolen women to their homes."

WOMEN AGRI- CUL- TURAL WORK- ERS

When the Red Army at last came winding around the mountain paths, its red banners flying, Ningkang went out to meet it. Even the shopkeepers and small merchants mingled with the crowds of welcome.

On that day there was a mass meeting in Ningkang, and to it came peasants and workers from the many villages beyond. It was a meeting far greater than a fair or greater than the crowds attending a wandering folk theatre. It was the birth of the mass revolutionary movement in the mountain regions beyond Chingkang-shan.

From the throngs of men and women at this meeting, committees were elected for the forming of unions and

China's Red Army Marches (New York: The Vanguard Press, 1934), pp. 54-58. The year was 1928 and the province was Kiangsi in southern China where Mao and Chu Teh would build a powerful Soviet. The destruction of this Soviet by Chiang Kai-shek led to the famous Long March of 1934-35.

mass organizations: Peasant League, Trade Union, Agricultural Laborers' Union, Women's Union. And in the days that followed, elected delegates from the new unions took their place as members of the Revolutionary Committee ruling the district—a Committee afterwards to be turned into a Soviet.

In this Ningkang district were thousands of women agricultural laborers with unbound feet. For their labor the landlords had paid them rice and four or five silver dollars a year. But some were slaves, bought for work on the land or in the rich homes.

When the Agricultural Laborers' Union was formed, these women agricultural laborers entered, dominating it, and when the Red Guards were organized, some of these women stepped forward, saying:

"Our feet are big—look! They have never been bound! We can walk and work like men! We are strong as the men! Give us guns!"

So the Red Guards of Ningkang became a mixed body of armed men and women with red bands on their sleeves.

There were also some two hundred women in the town who were knitters of stockings and underwear, working at primitive knitting machines owned by masters. There were also many weavers and spinners, some of them women. For such workers the daily hours of labor had been as many as fifteen or sixteen and they who worked in the shops had to act as servants if the master demanded it. There were many women who combined the care of their families with spinning, weaving, shoemaking, sandal and mat weaving, or with labor in the fields.

When these women saw the women agricultural workers organizing, they also demanded the right to join the Agricultural Laborers' Union. For it seemed to them to be a union of women. Before the Red Army had been in Ningkang one week, three thousand women insisted upon this right. But a general Women's Union was organized for them instead, and they took their first step in changing the conditions of women workers and in emancipating themselves from old customs and traditions.

Then Ningkang was swept by another new idea. The Communist Party that guided the mass organizations and that ruled the Red Army adopted a slogan calling for the confiscation without compensation of all land held by the landlords, the temples and clans, and its division amongst the toiling peasants.

So great was the enthusiasm of the peasants at this that many peasants began confiscating and dividing the land at once, the women agricultural laborers leading.

But when the confiscation and division of the land was formally discussed in the Peasant Leagues, things did not go so well. The class struggle began to appear. For not only were poor and middle peasants in these Leagues, but there were rich peasants also. The rich peasants employed hired agricultural laborers, and sometimes rented out land to tenants. Many of them could read and write, and because of this they became leaders in mass meetings or in the Peasant League. In public elections they proposed each other as committee members in the Peasant Leagues. Poor peasants, serfs, slaves, lifting their eyes from the earth for the first time, said of them:

"Good, let him be on the committee! I am poor and stupid and do not know how to speak or to read the characters!"

Then, when the question of the division of the land came up, the rich peasants thrust out their chests and said:

"The Revolution is for equality. This means that each person has the right to the same amount of land."

Now this meant that each member in a family, whether he be an old man or a baby, should be given the same amount of land.

Now and then a poor peasant or land laborer listening to the rich peasants bitterly remarked:

"*Ai-yo!* The clever bird chooses the branch on which to perch!"

The members in the family of the poor peasants were few. Most of their children died of the destitution of peasant existence while still at the mother's breast. Those who lived were few, and of these the sons had wandered off to the towns or coastal cities, seeking coolie labor, or even entering the armies of the militarists. And the girls had been sold as slaves. In the family of a poor peasant were two or three, or perhaps four souls at best. But the members of a rich peasant family were many, for the richer a man the more chances his children had of survival, the more certain it was that brothers and sons did not wander as coolies to the cities looking for the labor that horses and machines do in other lands.

The poor peasants were as yet no equal for the rich. The slogan for the division of the land aroused in them such burning hopes that they were as if intoxicated. However the land was divided, it would be better than their old servitude. If they should be given five *mou* of land, it would seem much.

True, it aroused their bitterness that the rich peasants owned twenty, thirty, and even fifty *mou*. The rich peasants were in fact small landlords and only the fact that they had wormed their way into the Peasant Leagues saved them from the fate of the landlords. Cunningly they trimmed their sails to the winds of the Revolution. Around Ningkang the land of the landlords was confiscated and divided according to the number of mouths in the family. The poor peasants and land laborers got a little, some five *mou* of good land, some six or seven of medium. But the rich peasants kept all they had, and took still more.

The poor peasants complained after the division had taken place. For the rich peasants also still employed agricultural laborers. They also owned animals and agricultural implements and would allow no other man to use them, saying they needed them for themselves. Through the minds of some of the poor swept waves of hatred. Others said one should be satisfied with what the gods had magnanimously given. And the rich peasants in the Peasant Leagues would even have it appear that they themselves had given land to the poor. And so many were the problems of the masses, so severe the tasks of the Red Army, so heavy the burden of the Communist Party, that in these early days of the agrarian revolution the problem of land division remained undetermined.

The Red Army remained in Ningkang until middle April. Through the spring rice rains it had made sallies into distant market towns, scattering the White troops, capturing bullets, confiscating rice from the rich merchants. On the homes of the rich landlords the Political Department had left proclamations saying:

"To the masses of .... town! On this day the Red Army of Workers and Peasants, the vanguard of the Chinese Revolution, has confiscated the following from the rich who oppress and loot the poor: 500 *piculs* of rice, 100 *piculs* of salt, 25 hams, 5,000 dollars in silver, 20 lengths of white cloth, 150 flashlights with batteries, machinery for making bullets, 36 cases of medicine. The Red Army has taken nothing from the workers or peasants, nothing from the small traders. Signed: Political Department of the Red Army, April 12, 1928."

It was in the second week of April that couriers came from the north, bearing the news of the approach of the

Red Army led by Mao Tse-tung. They would await Chu Teh's forces at the foot of Chingkang mountain.

The bugles sounded over the town. Yu-kung blew his bugle with a gusto that almost made the leaves on the trees tremble. Then leaving one company of Red Army men behind to reënforce the Red Guards of Ningkang, the Army began to march toward Chingkangshan. It looked clean and rested. Its clothing had been washed and patched by the "sewing-cutting" corps of women and girls of Ningkang, and its feet clad in new straw sandals. With its red banners flying, it swung along the hillside paths, over the mountains toward the peaks of Chingkangshan.

THE
WOMEN
TAKE
A HAND

When I first met old Mother Tsai, she had already emerged as a leader of the women in the valley. She was unusually tall for a "south Yangtze Valley" woman; her skin was brown, and the veins on her old hands stood out like ridges on a hillside. She was thin and hard, and when she spoke, her voice was firm and almost harsh. Her hair, touched with white, was drawn back from a high forehead and rolled in a knot at the nape of her neck. As a peasant woman and the mother of many sons, she had suffered bitterly all her life, but of this she never spoke. Her white cotton jacket was neatly buttoned up close around the neck and her dark cotton trousers always seemed to have just been washed. Though none of these people ever ironed their clothing,

Battle Hymn of China, pp. 270-72. This story draws on Smedley's experiences among the guerillas in southern China in late 1938. An earlier version appeared as "No Sacrifice . . . No Victory" in *Vogue*, April 15, 1942, pp. 48-49, 87.

hers must somehow have been pressed beneath some weight. She was the embodiment of dignity and staunchness.

It was difficult to believe that she was sixty-eight, for she seemed much younger. She was, she told me, a widow with four children. Of her three sons, the two elder were in the New Fourth Army, and the younger, a boy of fifteen, helped her and her daughters-in-law till the fields.

Before the war, life in the villages had been drab and monotonous. But when the New Fourth Army had marched into the valley the year before, the world had seemed to enter with it. Many girl students had joined the Political Department of the Army; when they went knocking on the doors of the village women, the old world had crumbled. The ladies of the gentry had refused to receive them, sending their menfolk instead, and thus suggesting that the girls were prostitutes. But when the girls knocked on Mother Tsai's door, she looked into their eyes and knew they were not bad. She invited them in, placed bowls of tea before them, and called her daughters-in-law and neighbor women to come and sit with them. And in this way the Women's National Salvation Association was born in the valley. It grew until it had over a hundred members.

Mother Tsai's lean, tall figure could often be seen walking along the paths from village to village, urging women to join literacy classes, and attend discussion groups to learn what the war was about and how they could help. After the day's work was done, women could be seen sitting on their doorsteps, cutting out pieces of cloth and sewing. When I asked them what they were doing, they replied: "Making shoes for the Army."

More and more women took over the field work previously done by men. The younger men had joined the Army and the older men and boys helped in the

fields or carried supplies to the battlefield and brought
back the wounded. On every festival day members of
the Women's Association would go to the hospital to
"comfort the wounded" with gifts of food, sing songs,
and talk with the soldiers. It was always Mother Tsai
who delivered the speeches in the wards, telling the
wounded that they were all her sons and the sons of the
Women's Association. And she never closed a speech
without telling them about women's rights, or urging
them to induce their womenfolk to join the Association.
Some men had never heard such talk before and they
listened with respect. About such matters Chinese men
everywhere seemed much more civilized and tolerant
than Occidental men, and only a few ever opposed the
new movement.

The women had become particularly confident after
Army women had conducted classes. One of these
classes covered Japanese espionage and sabotage
methods in the war zones and it urged women to
become the "eyes and ears of the Army," to combat
defeatism, watch everywhere for spies or traitors, and
boycott Japanese goods. One phrase covered all such
activities: "Guarding the rear of our Army." After that
they never just sat and listened while their menfolk
dispensed wisdom; they took part in conversations,
conducted propaganda about almost everything on
earth, went to mass meetings, and questioned every
stranger who passed through the valley about his family
and his family's family down to the tenth generation.

Now and then a man rose to protest against the "new
women." There was, for instance, the merchant Chang,
who declared that, when the women got going, they
wore out men and exhausted horses. Mother Tsai was
the worst of all, he said, and an idea in her head rattled
like a pea in an empty gourd. She had become
particularly obnoxious to him since she had discovered

that he was buying up all the small white beans from the lah tree. The people made candles from these beans, but Chang had begun cornering them and selling them in Wuhu. Now, the city of Wuhu had been occupied by the Japanese, and the women soon wanted to know just why any person traded in it. How was it, they asked, that Merchant Chang could pass through the Japanese lines, month in and month out, without difficulty? And why had the wax beans of the valley suddenly found such a big market? Perhaps the Japanese made oil from them! No one respected Merchant Chang anyway, for everyone knew that he had a hand in the valley's new opium-smoking den, where the village riff-raff and even some family men had begun squandering their money.

Mother Tsai one day walked straight into Chang's shop and put the question to him. With withering contempt, the merchant asked her if *she* wanted to buy his beans. This was not only an insult, but it mocked the poverty of the old lady and of every peasant family in the valley. Merchant Chang soon learned what it meant to despise the will of the people. Not a soul would buy or sell him anything, and when he passed through the streets people looked the other way. Once a little boy threw a stone after him and called out: "Traitor." And one day as he passed a farmhouse, he distinctly heard a dog being set on him.

At last Merchant Chang went in anger to the local government official. The official called in Mother Tsai for a friendly talk. The old lady went, but not alone. The entire membership of the Women's Association escorted her to the official's door, and her son, her daughters-in-law, and several relatives accompanied her right into his home. Other villagers trailed along and it looked as if the whole village was waiting outside the official's residence. The official himself was not a bad fellow. In fact, he was patriotic and liberal-minded. But when he saw the crowd, he became more liberal-minded than ever. He asked Mother Tsai to explain her talk with Chang, and she told him about the traffic with Wuhu and about the opium and gambling den. The opium, she pointed out, came from some corrupt officers in a provincial Chinese army farther to the west. There had never before been an opium-smoking den in the valley, and the Women's Association asked that it be closed down.

The official admitted the evil of opium and gambling, but said there was no law against either. A new opium-smoking law was expected soon; until then he urged the women to argue with the men "with love in their hearts." Old Mother Tsai replied: "We women have already argued with love in our hearts. The men will not listen. They tell us to go back to our kitchens and not interfere in men's affairs."

Mother Tsai ended the interview by announcing to the amazed official: "We women have risen. We will not allow rich men to despise the will of the people."

Nor could the official do anything about Merchant Chang. There was no proof that he traded with the Japanese. True, he replied, men had seen him in the streets of Wuhu. But he might have slipped through the Japanese lines like other men. There was no law against this.

March 8 brought matters to a crisis. This was always celebrated throughout China as International Women's Day and the valley buzzed with preparation for a mass meeting in the great courtyard of an old ancestral temple. Men leaders had been invited to say a few words of greeting, but it was a woman's day. All the front seats in the temple courtyard were reserved for women, while soldiers, officers and civilian men were invited to sit in the back. The faces and names of the women scientists, writers and revolutionary leaders of many nations shouted at us from scores of posters. A number of them called on the women to "revive the spirit of Florence Nightingale."

On this morning Mother Tsai led the entire Women's National Salvation Association to the Army hospital to present gifts to the wounded. Before going to the wards, they called to present me with ten eggs and a chicken. Mother Tsai sat very straight and asked me to tell Western women how the women of China had struggled to emancipate themselves. "You," she said, "express the high spirit of womanhood by your willingness to eat bitterness with us." I was deeply affected by her tribute.

I went with the women to the hospital wards and watched them bring in great bamboo baskets filled with eggs, cakes and half a slaughtered hog. Their husbands proudly carried the gifts down the aisles for the wounded to see and exclaim over. And when this was done, all the women gathered and sang the *Consolation for the Wounded* song, telling the soldiers, "O men of honor," that they had "suffered the wounds of war for millions of women and children."

It was a beautiful and moving scene. After it was finished, I talked with Mother Tsai and her followers. They wished to know what else they could do to help the wounded, and I proposed that they make pillows and pillow-cases, embroidering each case with such slogans as "Hero of the Nation" or "Toward the Final Victory." They accepted the idea eagerly and I started the campaign with a donation of money for cloth and silk thread, assuring them that they must not thank me, that this was my fight as well as theirs.

The mass meeting that afternoon was a tremendous success. Mother Tsai had an attack of stage fright, but conquered her fear and went on to speak of women's rights and their part in the war. Before finishing, she announced that her Association was going to root out all evils in the valley, including gambling and opium and idleness. In concluding she revealed that news had just reached her that one of her own sons had been wounded at the front. It was an honor to be the mother of a man who had suffered in such a cause, she said, and it made her own duty so much the greater.

She was about to leave the stage, but halted to stare. For all the soldiers and commanders had risen and were holding their rifles high in the air. To the stirring strains of the *Volunteer Marching Song* the old lady moved slowly off the stage.

A few days later one of the Army doctors called me out to the out-patient clinic of the hospital, and to my amazement I found old Mother Tsai lying injured on a stretcher. As I bent over her, she began in a weak voice to tell me what had happened. It was all about the opium and gambling den, she said. The Women's Association had argued with the men to close it down, and when they had refused, she and the other women had stalked into the place and peremptorily ordered the men to go home. The ruffians had shouted abuse at them. Finally Mother Tsai had brought a big stick down across the table, scattering all the money and mah-jong cubes around the room. Other women had started to follow suit, the men had fought them, and there had been a great row. Almost every woman had been beaten—Mother Tsai worst of all.

For days the valley was in an uproar. Fathers, husbands, and sons, soldiers and commanders stalked about in a fury. Mother Tsai's bed was surrounded by a crowd of women, every one of them with some sort of bruise, but all of them chattering happily. For the opium den had been closed down and Merchant Chang and every man who had beaten a woman had been jailed. "A great victory—a great victory," the women kept saying.

Old Mother Tsai appealed to me:

"Now, American comrade, write to the American Woman's National Salvation Association and tell them about this. Tell about our victory and tell them that without sacrifice there can be no victory."

I think my voice trembled a little as I said I would do that, but I sat thinking of American women—women well clad and well cared for, convinced by a thousand movies that "love" was the solution of all problems. I doubted whether many of them could appreciate the conditions under which Chinese women lived and struggled.

It was a few weeks before Mother Tsai was back on the field of battle. One day I glanced up from my desk and found her standing in the door, a small group of young women behind her—all smiling. I went outside with them and found men, women, and children carrying pillows. Each pillow-case was embroidered with flowers and birds, and across each stretched such a slogan as I had suggested. Later the women went from bed to bed, presenting each man with a pillow. The surprise and pleasure of the patients was payment enough.

There were too few pillows, however, for several wounded men had just come in, including two Japanese prisoners of war. Promising to make others for them, Mother Tsai induced two Chinese soldiers to surrender their pillows to these Japanese. With the presentation, she delivered a speech about the rights of women. The Japanese gazed up at her with amazed and embarrassed smiles.

"It's grand, simply grand," I exclaimed to a doctor. "The old lady has the Japanese on their backs, and they can't do a thing but lie there and listen to her talk about the equality of women. What a dose for them! Just what they deserved!"

MY CHI- NESE SON

When I first reached the Storm Guerrilla Detachment of the New Fourth Army, a *hsiao kwei* or "little devil," was assigned to serve me as orderly. The woman reporter who accompanied me was similarly provided. Although this was the custom of the guerrilla armies, I still had to face an old problem—not only of having a child serve me, but of exposing children to battle.

Children have taken part in people's revolutions in all lands and in all periods. They had taken part in China's 1911 revolution and in the "great revolution" of 1925-27. When the civil wars began in China in 1927, the rising Red Army had faced this problem on a mass scale, for thousands of young boys entered their ranks

Battle Hymn of China, pp. 463-75. Li Hsien-nien (the New Fourth Army commander mentioned toward the end) is now a vice-premier of the People's Republic of China. An earlier version of this story appeared as "After the Final Victory" in *Asia*, February 1942, pp. 119-22.

and sometimes whole families of men, women and children fought with the soldiers.

As in the main New Fourth Army, these children were given such light work as bringing hot water each morning, keeping clean the room of an officer or political leader, and carrying messages. For a number of hours each day they had to study reading and writing or attend classes. From orderly they "graduated" to guard or soldier, and many of them later became commanders in the field. With them an entirely new force entered Chinese society—a force that had grown up in a world of war and was literally rooted in revolutionary consciousness.

In many ways this was a sad phenomenon, yet I could see no other path for these children to follow. If Army life was too rigorous for children, it was still not half so bad as their fate in factories and small workshops. With the exception of those in well-to-do families, China's children bore the brunt of all the storms of misfortune that swept the country.

Time and again I heard foreigners in China declare that the *hsiao kwei* in the guerrilla armies were kept by the officers for homosexual purposes. These were stories invented by diseased minds. It may be said that I am naive or that I was lied to; but few things can be hidden in an army: its life is communal; it is, in truth, the greatest goldfish-bowl of them all. There is absolutely nothing that Chinese soldiers do not gossip about; war conditions them to utter frankness, and even if one man lies to you, the next will tell you the truth.

The *hsiao kwei* assigned to me was typical of most of the "little devils" who joined the guerrillas. His name was Shen Kuo-hwa, and though he said he was ten or eleven years old—he did not know which—he looked much younger. With that curious wisdom of China's children, he told me that he was small because he had never had enough to eat and had been sick so much when he was a "beggar boy." That was long ago, he explained, when he was "very little." Bandits had fallen upon his poor home in Honan, burning it to the ground, killing his father, and injuring his mother. His two elder brothers had both joined the Army to make a living, and after this disaster he had become a beggar boy to earn money to support himself and his mother.

He could not remember how old he had been at that time. His mother had told him to take a bowl and stand in front of a rich man's house. So he had toddled out and stood before a big house all day long. Since he did not know how to whine and cry out or beat his head in the dust, no one paid the least attention to him. Only at the end of the day did a man who was coming out of the house ask him why he didn't go home. Kuo-hwa told the man that his house had been burned, his father killed, and his mother hurt. He himself was a beggar, he explained. The man gave him some coppers and sent him away.

When the snow fell and the wind howled, the woman reporter and our two little orderlies often remained in my room all day long because I was one of the few persons in the detachment for whom a charcoal fire was provided. Like every soldier in the detachment, the two children had lice. One day I decided to delouse them. While they bathed in a small wooden tub in the corner of the room, I heated the fire tongs red-hot in the coals, then drew them down the wet inner seams of their uniforms. When Kuo-hwa had bathed, he came up in all his naked innocence and stood by the table watching me, talking all the while about the years before he joined the guerrillas.

"All the *lao pai hsing* (common people) have lice in winter time," he said. "I had them when I was a beggar boy and when I worked for the big landlord. If you have just a few lice, you have to scratch all the time. But if you have very many you no longer itch, but get a headache which does not go away. Yesterday another soldier died of this louse sickness. While he was dying many, many lice crawled off his body into the straw."

Kuo-hwa took the lack of medical care entirely for granted. When he had been a beggar boy, he said, he himself had often been ill. He would simply lie down somewhere until he felt better. Sometimes people had set their dogs on him, and one dog had bitten him on his leg, leaving a long scar.

"I'm afraid of dogs," he added. "I'm afraid they'll catch me." He had a scar on his left cheek, but that was a result of the time when the bandits had burned down his home.

Having no conception of time, Kuo-hwa did not know how long he had been a beggar. He had watched the "rich little boys" go to school, because they had thrown stones at him. He wanted to study, but found he could not because he was not "rich." By tracing in the dust the inscriptions he saw on scraps of paper he had learned to write such simple things as "one, two, three," but after that the numerals were too difficult. When he had asked people to teach him to write his name, they had laughed and asked why a beggar boy should want to learn to write. He had learned to write his name only after he had joined the guerrillas.

He must have been about six years old when his mother got a small landlord to guarantee him to a big landlord as a reliable cow herd. The landlord paid him eighty Chinese cents a year and gave him food, shelter, and the coats and trousers occasionally thrown away by his own sons. When he was paid each New Year's, the child gave his mother the eighty cents, and she bought cloth and made him the shoes he used during the winter.

When I was finished delousing Kuo-hwa's uniform, he

put it on. Then he said to me: "You are both my father and my mother."

I drew him to me, held him between my knees, combed his hair, and helped him button his jacket. This embarrassed him a little, for no one had ever done it before. He was supposed to take care of me, not I of him.

The Army was everything to Kuo-hwa, it was his Rock of Ages, and he gave it credit for everything he had learned. But, he explained, he had not been with it very long—only a year now—and thus he had a great deal still to learn. Listening to him talk, with his small melancholy face turned up to me, the woman reporter exclaimed in a low voice: "What an existence!"

As Kuo-hwa talked, the wind wailed outside. He went to the window and peeked through the hole in the paper stretched across the frame. The storm would not last long now, he assured us, for when the wind sounded like that and the snow lay on the earth as it did, the storm would soon stop. That he had learned by watching many storms while he worked for the rich landlord.

We asked him how he had come to join the guerrillas. He had once been sent into Kioshan, on the Peking-Hankow railway, he said, and had stopped to watch an army of soldiers march through. Then suddenly he had seen one of his brothers among them! But this had been his "bad brother," he explained, his "good brother" having been killed in the battle at Marco Polo Bridge at the beginning of the war. His "bad brother" talked with him, but would not give him or his mother any money. Instead, he called Kuo-hwa a fool for working for eighty cents a year and advised him to get a job that paid good money.

From the soldiers Kuo-hwa had heard talk about the Eighth Route Army. It was a good Army, a poor man's Army, the soldiers said. Officers could not beat or curse the soldiers, and everyone learned to read and write and there were clubs and singing groups. Kuo-hwa asked where he could find this "poor man's Army" because, he explained to the soldiers, he himself was a poor man and would like to join it. They laughed at him and told him the Army was far, far away. So he went out and asked a policeman, but the man only shook him and said that the Eighth Route Army was made up of bandits.

Shortly after, he came across a bearded old soldier dressed in a shabby military uniform, and asked him the same question. The old soldier, named Wang Lao-han, also said that Kuo-hwa was too little to join an army, but that the Eighth Route was months away if you walked straight north. Then old Wang added that he himself came from a poor man's army and that it was not far away. It was the Storm Guerrilla Detachment. The old man laughed at Kuo-hwa's announcement that he was going to join the guerrillas. "Do you know," replied the old man, "that the guerrillas live a bitter life, with little food and poor clothing, that they march and fight all the time, and that sometimes they get no money at all?"

For one whole day Kuo-hwa dogged the footsteps of Wang, and all day long the little fellow pleaded his case: because of too little food and too much sickness he was smaller than he should be, but he didn't want to get rich and he could walk long distances and carry heavy burdens ... here the landlord's servants beat him and made him do much of their work ... and no one would help him write even his own name. ... Finally, at the end of the day, Wang Lao-han grew so weary that he said Kuo-hwa might go with him and try out the guerrilla life. Kuo-hwa followed him into the mountains, and since then he had been an orderly.

The woman reporter often sat with the two children, helping them with their lessons. Each of the boys had a small primer written and published by the detachment itself. It began with the words "man" or "human being," and went on to "worker," "peasant," and "soldier," then to the name of the Army, the name of the Japanese Army, and so on to sentences. Across the bottom of each page was a question for discussion. Some of these read:

"A peasant produces rice, a worker weaves cloth. Why can't the peasant eat the rice he produces and the weaver wear the clothes he weaves?" . . . "Why is there a distinction between the rich and the poor?" . . . "Why are both the rich and the poor anti-Japanese to-day?" . . . "What prevents human beings from relying on each other?" . . . "Why is the Japanese Army the most cruel on earth?"

It was such questions, I feel, that were accountable for much of the opposition to the Eighth Route and New Fourth Armies.

"When I grow up I want to join the cavalry and fight the Japanese," Kuo-hwa said to me more than once. And each time I thought of lice and typhus and wondered if he would live to become a man, to lead poor men into battle.

Soon I had an opportunity to join a platoon of troops going to join a field regiment in the lake regions to the northwest of Hankow. The woman reporter decided to go with me, but we both felt it would be dangerous to take our *hsiao kwei* with us. Yet when I thought of leaving them behind I could not shake off the memories of the lice and the relapsing fever that menaced them constantly. When I told Kuo-hwa that I was leaving, he seemed to be struggling to keep from crying. I could not endure it and wrote a request to the detachment commander asking for permission to take the child with me. Kuo-hwa took the message and shot away like a streak of light, but I later heard from the commander that he did not really deliver it. Instead, he popped into the room of the commander, saluted, and announced that I wanted him to go with me! The commander was somewhat surprised, but the boy stood his ground. He argued that he had often marched with the Army all night long, carrying heavy loads. Furthermore, he pleaded, I needed him because he knew all my habits and needs.

The commander replied that since I really wished it, Kuo-hwa could of course go with me. The child asked him to write this down, and soon came running back with the written permission. I was surprised, but thought that the Army knew what it was doing.

So I took Kuo-hwa with me into the lake regions. On the third night out we stopped at a village about five miles from the motor highway which we planned to cross at midnight. A group of new volunteers, as yet without arms, had gathered to join us in the village, and a number of travelers carrying bundles were also waiting for us; for the highway was used by the Japanese to send reinforcements up to the Ta Hung mountain front, and they had established garrisons in all the larger villages near by.

When the darkness was deep enough, we lined up to march. A number of peasants had gathered to see off their sons who had volunteered. I remember one old woman standing on a little knoll, wiping the tears from her eyes, and a young woman with a baby in her arms who kept running by the side of one of the men and crying: "Come back as soon as you can!" And then out of a house on the outskirts of the village we heard an Amazonian voice bawling the name of a youth. Before the woman reached us we were already marching rapidly, but she caught up with us and ran up and down the column, peering into the face of each man. We learned that her son had run away to join the guerrillas and she was trying to find him. But not a sound came from our marching column, and long after we had left her behind we heard her voice wailing in the night.

A few hours later we skirted the walls of a village, intending to cross the highway beyond, but just as we came within sight of the road, we stopped dead in our tracks. There, about a hundred yards ahead of us, were a dozen or more Japanese soldiers, rifles slung across their backs, standing around a huge bonfire in front of a building. As we watched, several Japanese came out of the building with tables and chairs and threw them on the fire. Then they all stood about, warming themselves contentedly.

We drew back behind the village walls and the guerrillas put their heads together and began whispering. The woman reporter and I joined them. They were planning to wipe out the Japanese! We both protested. We had just passed a Japanese garrison a mile away, we argued, and they would come out and attack us from the rear. We also pointed out that we did not know how many more Japanese were inside the house or what their equipment was. We had no more than twenty-five rifles and one machine-gun, and the machine-gun had only two dozen cartridges.

Finally we persuaded them to make a short detour and cut in toward the highway a few hundred yards away. The woman reporter and I were both riding our horses. Just as we approached the highway we heard the roar of approaching motor trucks. Immediately a wild whisper fled down the column ordering everyone to run and all non-fighters to get into the shelter of the hills. I saw the small figure of Kuo-hwa speeding across the highway ahead of me. In the darkness and confusion my horse dashed out to the end of a low, half-destroyed bridge, crouched and sprang. We landed on a road in the midst of figures scurrying in every direction. My muleteer grabbed the bit of my horse and ran toward the rice-fields. Ahead of me were three of the new volunteers in long gowns, running as I had seldom seen men run, and my muleteer kept whispering fiercely: "Beat the horse! Beat the horse! The enemy is coming!"

We went over an embankment in one leap and out over the dark fields, while from behind us bullets began singing to the stars, hand-grenades burst, and a machine-gun rattled. We heard the engines of enemy motor trucks grind to a stop, then one of them roar on down the highway.

"Stop!" I cried to the men. "The enemy isn't coming! We will get lost!"

"Beat the horse!" gasped the muleteer from behind me, and ran farther. I began to feel like a coward. We were abandoning our men, and I was the only one of our group with even a small pistol! I flung myself from the saddle and struggled with the terrified muleteer.

"We must go back! We must find our men!" I cried.

Through his hard breathing I heard the strange singing of the bullets.

"The devils! The devils!" he gasped, but ceased struggling. I grasped his hand and we led the horse behind the towering grave-mound of some rich man of old. Two of the volunteers had already disappeared.

The fighting had died down and all was as silent as the dead. There was no moon and only the stars gave a faint light. My horse began to champ the grass at our feet and the volunteer whispered: "Your horse is white and the enemy can see! He is eating grass and the enemy can hear!" With these words he turned and disappeared into the darkness.

My muleteer, now perfectly calm, whispered: "Now what?"

"Wait," I answered, and leaving him behind the grave-mound I crawled to the summit, lay down on my stomach, and in the darkness watched for any sign of movement. Nothing moved. Beyond was the dark outline of the hills along the highway. I strained my ears for any human sound: when none came I went down the hill and said: "I'll give the guerrilla signal."

"No! No!" cried the muleteer. "The devils may know it!"

"I *must*!" I said in desperation, and crawled up the hillock again, lay down, raised my hands, and clapped softly. No answer came back. I tried again, this time a little louder, and heard whispered protests behind me. No reply! I clapped again sharply, and from far away a cautious signal answered. I tried again and it was repeated. I grabbed my muleteer by the hand and my horse by the bridle and began to drag them in the direction of the signal. The muleteer kept saying: "It may be the enemy!" We moved forward, cautiously giving the signal at intervals and hearing the answer drawing ever nearer. Soon we were very near. We stopped short and stepped behind our horse. I drew out my pistol, released the safety catch, and waited.

Out of the darkness in front of us came three dark shadows. "Password!" they demanded harshly and we saw their rifles trained upon us.

"Asses!" cried the muleteer in wild joy, and ran toward them and fell upon their necks.

The three guerrillas slung their rifles back over their shoulders and, laughing, gave me pats of joy that almost knocked me down.

"We got 'em! We got 'em!" they cried, and holding hands, we walked across the rice-fields. One of them whistled softly in pure joy, broke off, and laughed: "Ai-yoh! When my hand-grenade landed right in the body of that truck, did the devils scatter! Did they scatter!" He turned to another and said: "Now listen here, remember that when a truck is running, you must not throw your hand-grenade right *at* it, but *ahead* of it! That's the reason we failed to get that first goddam truck!"

"Ta Ma Di!" the other cursed. "Of course our machine-gun had to jam! It couldn't wait until later. And of course we had to have only one."

Cursing the machine-gun and making uncomplimentary remarks about the mothers of Japanese soldiers, we finally reached a market town three miles from the highway. Here the Japanese had established a puppet government, but without troops, and every puppet was one of our men. The whole government came out to welcome us, and its chief stood in the midst of our troops talking excitedly.

As we came into the village I was surprised to see Kuo-hwa standing by like a lost soul. As soon as he saw me he ran to me, placed his two small hands on my arm, and stood in perfect silence looking up into my face. When the order had been given for us to scatter, he had fled with the woman reporter and a young poet, Loh Fan, who had become my assistant. But when he had learned that I had disappeared, he had begun running about in the darkness crying out, asking if the devils had caught me. The woman reporter had taken him by the hand and told him to be silent, but he had said that he *must* go and search for me, that I would answer to his voice, but no other. When they told him he was a child and would get lost, he ceased crying, looked around at the hills and trees, and answered: "I will find her and come back! When she came to our Army, they told me to serve her and said I must take care of her. It is my duty."

A heavy fog from the lakes that stretch for miles to the west and northwest of Hankow blanketed the earth, and at dawn we began marching onward through it. We passed villages from which all people had fled, thinking we might be Japanese clad in Chinese uniforms. As the light increased and the fog lifted we entered a market town on the shores of a great lake. Only three or four old men and women and a few children remained behind; all the rest of the population had rowed far out on the bosom of the lake. One of the old women took a huge brass gong, beat it, and bawled like a foghorn to the people on the lake: "Come back! Come back!"

They came back and gathered about us in joy, but their excitement was greatest when they saw me. They gathered about me in crowds and I heard men trying to decide whether I was a man or a woman, American, German, or English. One woman pulled back her little child in fear and declared: "She has eyes like a cat!"

My little Kuo-hwa could not endure this. He stood up before them and cried: "She does *not* have eyes like a cat! She is a woman and our American friend! She helps our wounded! In Tingjiachun she found a wounded man and fed him and gave him a bath. She even helped him do all his business."

The people turned their eyes on me in amazement. My "son" would not stop. "Look at her bandaged hand!" he demanded, taking my hand in his. "She got this when she picked up a pan of hot water while she was bathing a wounded soldier. She is both my father and my mother! If any of you are sick, she will cure you."

When at last I decided to leave the Storm Guerrillas, the thought of typhus or relapsing fever haunted me, and I decided to adopt Kuo-hwa as my son—if the detachment and he himself were willing. True, I argued with myself, he was not the only one. But in west China, I had learned, an American-trained professor of child education had established a school that laid great emphasis on science. The life was austere and the children did all their own work, and for relatively little money the children were well fed and clothed. I questioned very much the desirability of having a foreigner bringing up a Chinese child and perhaps thereby isolating him from his own people. Yet I allowed my mind to stray to some far-off time when I might be able to send Kuo-hwa to a foreign country for advanced scientific studies. But my own life was so dreadfully insecure and uncertain, dare I undertake such a project? I would try.

So I went to Li Hsien-nien, the commander of the Storm Guerrillas, and, while many men stood about, talked with him about adopting Kuo-hwa. Li had once been a Red Army commander and before that a carpenter; life had been bitter for him and for his people, and individuals must have seemed of little importance to him. When he asked me why I wished to adopt Kuo-hwa, I tried to give my reasons a scientific basis. The child had a scientific turn of mind, I argued, and I mentioned his observations of lice, of wind and snow, the way he learned to read and write so quickly, and how he could tell the directions from the stars at night. Good, Li Hsien-nien said, I could adopt the boy if I wished and if the boy himself consented.

A burly fellow leaning against the door-frame remarked that he could do all the things I said Kuo-hwa could do. And he felt certain that he knew much more about lice. Would I like to adopt him too? Li Hsien-nien smiled dryly and added that it wouldn't be a bad idea for me to adopt the whole lot of them! The conversation became a little rowdy.

But it was a very serious matter with Kuo-hwa. He asked me about the school in west China and said he was afraid of rich little boys. He belonged to the Army, he explained. I argued that he might try the school for a time, and then return to the Army and teach others what he had learned. The Army needed teachers, I urged. He thought in silence, then asked to be allowed to talk it over with the other little orderlies. The following day he came in with another orderly and gave me his decision.

"We think all men must remain at the front," he said. "You can adopt me after the final victory."

We could not sway him.

But before leaving the lake region I arranged for my "son" to join the Children's Dramatic Corps of the Storm Guerrillas. A young woman teacher was in charge of the corps, which spent half the day in study and the other half writing and rehearsing patriotic dramas, songs and folk-dances which were to be presented to soldiers and civilians.

As the small boat which was to take me out of the lake regions pulled away from the shore, I saw Kuo-hwa for the last time. He and two other boys stood on the bank, washing their clothes in the waters of the lake. He cried to me and waved, then stood perfectly still, watching as my boat disappeared into the mist.

A WHITE EPI-SODE

Down the Nine Level Pass leading to the south-east from Tungku walked a peasant girl and a barefoot peasant boy. The girl carried a small bundle of clothing done up in a large square blue cloth, and over the left arm of the boy hung a basket filled with eggs. The girl was very pretty and could have been no more than twenty-two. She was clad in a fresh blue jacket fastened high at the throat and reaching to her hips. The long black, full trousers reached to her strong ankles. Her head was bare and the thick black hair drawn back from a broad, smooth forehead and caught in a large smooth coil at the nape of her neck. Through the coil was a long, sin-

Red Flood Over China (Moscow: Co-operative Publishing Society of Foreign Workers, 1934), pp. 255-64. *Red Flood Over China* is a differently-edited version of *China's Red Army Marches*. The scene for this story is the Kiangsi Soviet area in southern China during the early 1930s. The White forces blockading the Soviet are Chiang Kai-shek's Nationalist troops.

gle-pronged pin made of hard bamboo, one end
sharpened to a dull point, the other broad and
decorated.

There was an undefinable gentleness, even wistfulness
in the large black eyes and in the whole body of the girl,
and only if one looked closely could one discern the
reason. Then one could see that perhaps within her
body a new life was taking form, and it must be a life
conceived in love, for only such could give to her face
that gentle, wistful dreaming.

But it was also clear that she was not just a girl who
dreamed and talked within her heart to the growing life
within her body. For her eyes were alert and intelligent
and her head turned quickly at every noise in the dense
forests overhanging the mountain path. And often her
hand reached up and unconsciously touched the
bamboo pin in her hair, as if something lay concealed
there.

Only three people knew the secret of that bamboo
pin. One was herself, another the comrade in the
Communication Department of the Red Army in
Tungku, and the other her young peasant husband,
Kung-liao, commander of a company in the Red Army.
They knew that within the hollow tube of the pin was a
colorless liquid, an invisible writing ink, and within this
a very fine brush with which she could write. They also
knew of the reason for her trip to Kian, and of the letter
she carried in the little bundle of clothing.

That letter would be her passport through the lines of
White troops surrounding the mountain of Tungku. The
envelope was addressed to her. Inside, the letter was
dated Kian and read as if from her husband, a clerk in
the shop of a silk merchant in the White stronghold.
"Leave that region of Red bandits at once," it read. "Go
to your grandmother in Pi-tan, and after that make your
way to Kian. I fear always for your life and honor in
such a dangerous Red region."

"You can make it?" her husband Kung-liao and the comrade in the Communication Department asked the girl.

"Have I not worked for two years and come through many bad experiences?" she asked proudly. "Now, more than ever before, they will not trouble me."

They knew what she meant. That she was an expectant mother would serve her well.

The girl thought of all these things as she passed down the Nine Level Pass, talking to the boy by her side. She glanced down at him, so thin and brown, padding along in his bare brown feet by her side. His wisp of jacket, open in the front, revealed the lean, hard body of a peasant lad no more than thirteen years of age. The threadbare gray trousers just reached the knees and were held up by a broad cloth girdle. She did not know, but she felt certain that in that girdle was his tiny stub of a pencil and the soft roll of bamboo paper. He was a clever boy and had learned to read and write in the Red Army school in Chintang. For four months he had gone far and wide for the Red Army, selling his eggs, collecting information.

His face was lifted to her as he spoke. A thin, serious face, at times almost solemn. The chin was soft and childish, the cheek-bones high. A pair of very bright, intelligent eyes, oblique and narrow, smiled up at her.

"You are never afraid, *Di-di*?" the girl asked him.

"Afraid, no. Once they caught me not far from Chintang and beat me. I said I was an orphan boy and the Reds had destroyed my home and killed my father and mother. I am alone and poor and have nothing to eat and must sell eggs to earn money for rice. The eggs are very costly, but that is because I am very poor . . . brothers, buy my eggs, I told them.

"I kept saying this and at last they believed and I went among them selling my eggs. I was new in the Red Army school then and did not know all the kinds of guns. But I knew the flags of the different White units and I knew some of the makes of guns. I counted the sentries and saw where they were posted. . . . Now I can read many characters and write down what I see that I may not forget. . . . When I grow older I will know more. . . . I will be like Comrade Mao—you know, silent and watchful, but always thinking and planning inside his mind."

The boy spoke solemnly, glancing up at the girl. Their eyes met, bright and enthusiastic, like youth advancing to meet the day.

"You are not afraid?" the boy asked the girl.

"Sometimes—when I meet the officers. Or White soldiers who have been mercenaries of the Generals for many years. They are like animals."

"But we will fight on!"

"Yes, we will fight on!"

Suddenly the boy halted in the path and said: "I will now go to the north around the base of that cliff. Good-bye, Comrade elder sister."

"Good-bye, *Di-di*," she answered, and stood watching him until he vanished in the thick shrubs obscuring the narrow path at the base of the cliff. Then she went down the pass.

From the base of the pass she could see in the distance the low roofs of the village of Lungfung and the wooden drawbridge over the river. She knew the village was deserted and all the peasants living in the hills or in Tungku. Only White soldiers were in the valley, guarding the drawbridge.

A group of about a dozen soldiers on the drawbridge watched her as she came near. Anxiously she approached. Two were sentries with guns, the others unarmed, squatting on their heels, tossing coppers. They stood up as she approached. Her heart seemed to stop beating for she saw they were older men with the unconscious faces of mercenaries. The sentry wore three gold rings on one hand.

"Who are you? Where do you come from?" one of the sentries asked roughly.

"My name is Lai-in. I am running away from Tungku and going to my husband in Kian. My husband is afraid of the Red bandits. Here is the letter from him."

She gave a long envelope with red lines on its face. The sentry took it but did not look at it. The other men crowded about, took the envelope and began turning it over and over. They drew out the enclosure and pretended to read, though they could not.

"Are there Red bandits in the mountains?" a sentry asked her.

"I do not know. There may be some. That is the reason my husband wants me to come to Kian."

One of the soldiers began pretending he could read the letter. A broad grin spread over the faces of the other men. He was reading lewd phrases about the intimacies of sexual relationship. The reading became rougher and the girl threw her hands before her burning face.

"That is not in my letter!" she cried. "Give me my letter!"

One of the men reached out and grasped her by the arm. She jerked free.

"Why wear your girdle so tight?" he asked, throwing his arms about her and kissing her violently on the mouth. The men roared and Lai-in struck out and hit the man in the face.

"You would have us believe you ain't been there before!" the man angrily exclaimed.

"Come with me," the sentry said, grinning into her face. "I'll read the letter in the pavilion." He grasped her by the arm and dragged her after him towards a little rest pavilion set back from the path. The other men trailed after him laughing at her struggling. One threw an arm about her, half-carrying her along.

Inside the pavilion they began to argue as to who should have her first. In terror she saw them begin tossing coins to decide. Her throat seemed to close up and her mouth became as dry as parchment.

She began to strike at the man who came toward her. The others laughed while he ripped the clothing from her, stripping her naked. She fought but he grasped her by the arm, giving it a vicious jerk backward. A fierce pain shot up her arm and through her whole body and darkness blinded her eyes. She felt someone tearing down her coil of hair, and instinctively she grasped at the precious bamboo pin. Then complete darkness overwhelmed her.

The men raped her one by one. Then she lay outstretched on the dirty pavilion floor, her tangled hair mixed with the dirt. One arm lay outstretched, crooked, torn. About her mouth was a fringe of foamy blood.

One of the soldiers kept staring down at her naked body and chalky face. His eyes rested on the round mound of her stomach, at something that moved beneath as if in violent protest, then subsiding into quietness as complete as the body.

The sentry reached out and kicked the girl to see if she was dead. Then another man reached out with his foot and kicked her ribs playfully. But she lay stretched cold and still, the foam congealing about her lips.

"Can't leave the body here," one of the men said.

They picked up her torn clothing, tied it about her, and thrust the bamboo pin playfully through the knot. Then one of them carried her to the river bank, heaved and tossed her into the stream. The body splashed, gurgled and disappeared from view. It came up twice near the water's surface, the long black hair outspread like the dark wings of night.

The men bent over the bridge and watched for some

time, and then, when the body appeared no more, turned away. The sentries took their places on the bridge, the others squatted on their heels and continued tossing coins.

Beyond, the boy *Di-di* had emerged from the mountain path to the north, and began walking along a bordering hill path. He had taken but a few steps when from the top of the hill he heard a command.

"Halt!"

He glanced up and saw a White officer with a body-guard of five men approaching.

"Who are you?" the officer demanded with cold ferocity.

"My humble name is Nan-ju. I am going to the market at Siangpu to sell my eggs."

"You came down from Tungku?"

"I went to Tungku to buy eggs. They have good eggs there."

"How many Reds are there in Tungku?"

"I do not know. I did not look for Red soldiers."

"Come with me, you little Red liar! This is the second time this week you've come down from Tungku!"

The boy was surrounded by the guards. He walked calmly, his head high, his black eyes alert and unafraid. He saw they were leading him to a village deserted of all but White troops. Then down the dirty street, through a door, into a paved courtyard, where soldiers were sitting about on stone benches, and into a room beyond.

The officer talked with the other White officers who were smoking cigarettes. Near the window sat a group of four officers about a little square table, playing mah-jong. Little piles of silver dollars were near their elbows.

The two White officers began questioning Nan-ju, the men at the mah-jong table listening, smoking, throwing their cigarette stubs on the flour. Nan-ju repeated his story about the eggs. "I know nothing of the Reds in Tungku," he finally concluded.

"How can you go up and down the Tungku pass without the consent of the Red bandits?" an officer asked him furiously, reaching out and striking the basket of eggs from his arm.

"I only buy eggs," he answered.

One of the men stepped over and began to search him. The boy's girdle was ripped open. A tiny little stub of a pencil and a thin roll of bamboo paper rolled out.

The officer became livid. "You're a spy for the bandits!" He reached out and struck the boy a blow across the mouth and nose. Nan-ju staggered but caught himself and stood very still and silent. The soldiers in the courtyard gathered in the door to watch.

"Shoot the little illegitimate offspring of a turtle," one of the officers at the mah-jong table in the corner remarked, as calmly as if he were placing a cube on the table.

Nan-ju looked about at the faces of the enemy. He saw the soldiers standing in the door. They were peasants—such men desert to the Red Army when they know why the masses fight, he thought. Then he turned to the officers and said:

"It is you who are the bandits! You are the enemies of the people. You murder our parents and burn our homes and our crops. You are running dogs of the landlords and imperialists."

"That to stop your mouth with!" one of the officers erupted, smashing him directly in the teeth. For a few minutes the boy could not see, then he felt something warm and salty in his mouth. He reached up and his hand filled with blood. He heard a command given, then someone grabbed him by the arm and he was again marching down the dirt street. Suddenly he found himself standing on a little grave mound right outside the village walls. Before him was a squad of soldiers, their guns pointing at him. Beyond them he saw the green heights of Tungku. Up there was the Red Army of workers and peasants, his father a commander in the Red Army.

"Ten thousand years to the Red Army!" he cried in a high childish voice.

A volley of shots rang out. The slender brown body jerked from the shock, then sank to the earth as if it were very, very sleepy. A little stream of blood flowed from beneath his body, joined another, and sank into the hungry grave.

The squad of soldiers stood at attention. One turned his head and caught the eye of a man by his side. Something in the looks of each other's faces held them as if spellbound. Another soldier stared at the body of the boy as if transfixed, his throat working convulsively.

Then the soldiers marched down the dirt street again, through the door and into the stone courtyard. They broke ranks and sat down on the stone benches, avoiding each other's eyes, staring at the flagstones beneath their feet. One of the men finally said in a low voice:

"Did you hear what he said?"

"Yes—they all say that."

"He was not afraid to die."

"No—they are all like that."

The other men listened in silence, hardly breathing.

"Why are the Reds not afraid to die—even their children are without fear."

"Because—because—well, you heard what he said. It is we who are the criminals—running dogs of the landlords and imperialists!"

One of the White officers heard the low voices and came to the door and stood staring out. He stood watching with thin hard lips. Then the soldier who had spoken stood up, hoisted his trousers with a defiant jerk, and left the courtyard. Another arose and followed him as if of urgent physical necessity. The officer watched them go in silence, glanced at the other men for some minutes, then returned in fury to the inside room.

In the window the four officers continued to play mah-jong. The little piles of silver dollars were at their elbows and they smoked, tossing the cigarette stubs on the floor.

SHAN-FEI, COMMU-NIST

This is the story of Shan-fei, daughter of a rich land-owner of Hunan, China. Once she went to school and wore silk dresses and had a fountain pen. But then she became a Communist and married a peasant leader. In the years that followed she—but I will begin from the beginning—

Her mother is the beginning. A strange woman. She was old-fashioned, had bound feet, and appeared to bow her head to every wish of her husband who held by all that was old and feudal. Yet she must have been rebellious. She watched her sons grow up, go to school, and return with new ideas. Some of these new ideas were about women—women with natural feet, who

Chinese Destinies: Sketches of Present-Day China, pp. 35-42. Shan-fei's story was recorded in the early 1930s. It first appeared in the *New Masses*, May 1931, pp. 3-5.

153

studied as men did, who married only when and whom they wished.

When her sons talked the mother would sit listening, her eyes on her little daughter, Shan-fei, kicking in her cradle. And long thoughts came to her. What those thoughts were we do not know—but we know that at last she died for the freedom of her daughter.

This battle was waged behind the high stone walls that surrounded her home. The enemy was her husband and his brothers. And the mother's weapons were the ancient weapons of subjected women: tears, entreaties, intrigue, cunning. At first she won but one point: her husband consented to Shan-fei's education, provided the teacher was an old-fashioned man who came to the home and taught only the Chinese characters. But Shan-fei's feet must be bound, and she must be betrothed in marriage according to ancient custom. So the child's feet were bound and she was betrothed to the weakling son of a rich neighbor, a corrupt old man with many concubines.

Until Shan-fei was eleven years old, her father ruled as tyrants rule. But then he suddenly died. Perhaps it was a natural death, and perhaps Shan-fei's mother wept sincere tears. Yet the funeral was not finished before the bandages were taken off the feet of the little girl, and the earth on the grave was still damp when Shan-fei was put in a school one hundred *li* away.

But though the bandages were removed, the little feet had already been crippled by five years of binding, and the half-dead, useless toes remained bent under the feet like stones to handicap the girl throughout her life.

Anyway the bandages were gone, and with them the symbol of one form of enslavement. There remained the betrothal to the rich man's son. Such betrothals in China are legally binding, and the parents who break them can be summoned to court and heavily punished, just as if they had committed a dangerous crime. Shan-fei's mother, however, seemed to have tendencies that the feudal-minded ones called criminal. For she was suspected of plotting and intriguing to break the engagement.

Worse still, it was rumored that she did not advise Shan-fei to be obedient as girls should be but encouraged her to be free and rebellious. This rumor spread like fire when the news came that Shan-fei had led a students' strike against the corrupt administration of her school. She was nearing sixteen at the time, the proper age for marriage. Yet she was expelled in disgrace from the school, and returned home with her head high and proud. And her mother, instead of subduing her, whispered with her alone, then merely transferred her to a still more modern school in far-away Wuchang on the Yangtze, where rumor further had it that she was becoming notorious as a leader in the students' movement. Moreover, men and women students studied together in Wuchang.

Things became so bad that at last the rich landlord filed a legal suit against Shan-fei's mother and summoned her to court, charged with plotting to prevent the marriage. But the old lady defended herself most cunningly and even convinced the court that all she desired was a postponement of the marriage for another two years.

She convinced the judge—but not the landlord. And, as was the custom, he called to his aid the armed gentry of the countryside; when Shan-fei returned home from her vacation that year, they made an attempt to capture her by force. They failed and Shan-fei escaped and remained in Wuchang for another year. When she came home again, her capture was again attempted. With the aid of her mother she again escaped, hid in the homes of peasants, and returned by devious ways to Wuchang.

When she reached Wuchang, however, the news of her
mother's death had preceded her. Perhaps this death was
also natural—perhaps not. Shan-fei says it was—that her
mother died from the misery of the long-drawn-out
struggle and family feud. "She died for my sake," she
says, and in her manner is no trace of tearful sentimen-
tality, only a proud inspiration.

Shan-fei's school comrades tried to prevent her from
going home for the funeral. But this was more than the
death of a mother—it was the death of a pioneer for
woman's freedom. And Shan-fei, being young and
unafraid and a bit proud that she had escaped the old
forces twice, thought she could defeat them again. Lest
anything should happen, she laid plans with her school
comrades in the Students' Union that they should look
for her and help her escape if she did not return to
Wuchang within a certain period.

The body of the old mother had scarcely been laid to
rest when Shan-fei's ancestral home was surrounded by
armed men and she was violently captured and taken to
her father-in-law's home, where she was imprisoned in
the bridal suite and left to come to her senses. She did
not come to her senses but, instead, starved for one
week. Her hunger strike was broken only by another
woman rebel within the landlord's family.

This woman was the first wife of the landlord, whom
the Chinese call "Mother" to distinguish her from his
concubines. The old lady watched and listened to this
strange, rebellious rich girl, around whom a battle had
been waged for years, and also used the ancient wiles of
a woman to gain the girl's freedom. This freedom,
granted by the landlord, meant only the right to move
about the home and the compound but did not extend
beyond the high surrounding walls.

In China, however, few or no secrets can be kept, and
news travels on the wind. Perhaps that is how one girl

and two men students from Wuchang happened to come to the neighborhood and bribed a servant to carry messages to Shan-fei. Finally, one late evening Shan-fei mounted the wall by some means and disappeared into the dusk on the other side. That night she and her friends rode by starlight toward Wuchang.

This was the late summer of 1926, and China was swept by winds of revolution. Soon the southern armies lay siege to Wuchang. And Shan-fei gave up her studies and went to the masses. She became a member of the Communist Youth, and in this work she met a peasant leader whom she loved and who was loved by the peasants. She defied the old customs that bound her by law to the rich landlord's son and announced her free marriage to the man she loved. And from that day down to the present moment her life has been as deeply elemental as are the struggles of mother earth. She has lived the life of the poorest peasant workers, dressed as they dress, eaten as they eat, worked as they work, and has faced death with them on many a battle-front. Even while bearing her unborn child within her womb, she threw all her boundless energy into the revolution; and when her child was born she took it on her back and continued her work.

In those days the Kuomintang and the Communist Parties still worked together, and, as one of the most active woman revolutionaries, Shan-fei was sent back to her ancestral home as head of the Woman's Department of the Kuomintang. There she was made a member of the Revolutionary Tribunal that tried the enemies of the revolution, confiscated the lands of the rich landlords and distributed them among the poor peasants. She helped confiscate all the lands of her own family and of the family of her former fiancé.

When the revolution became a social revolution, the Communists and the Kuomintang split, and the dread

White Terror began. The militarists and the feudal
landlords returned to power. Shan-fei's family and the
family of her fiancé asked the Kuomintang for her
arrest. And this order was issued. It meant death for
herself and her child. Two women and three men who
worked with her were captured, the women's breasts
were cut off, and all five were beheaded in the streets.
But the workers bored air-holes in a coffin, placed
Shan-fei and her baby inside, and carried them through
the heavily guarded gates of the city out into the
graveyard beyond the walls. From there she began her
journey to Wuchang. Once she was captured because her
short hair betrayed her as a revolutionary; but she
pleaded her innocence with her baby in her arms and
was released.

She reached the Wuchang cities only to be ordered by
the Communist Party to return to the thick of the fight
in western Hunan during the harvest struggle, when the
peasants armed themselves, refused to pay rent or taxes,
and began the confiscation of the lands. Shan-fei was
with them during the days; at night she slept in the
forests on the hills, about her the restless bodies of
those who dared risk no night in their homes. Then
troops were sent against them. The peasants were
defeated, thousands slain, and the others disarmed.

Again Shan-fei returned to Wuhan. And again she was
sent back to the struggle. This time, however, she went,
presumably as a Kuomintang member, to a city held by
the militarists. Beyond the city walls were peasant
armies. Inside Shan-fei worked openly as the head of the
Woman's Department of the Kuomintang; secretly, she
carried on propaganda amongst the troops and the
workers. Then in this city the chief of the judicial
department met her and fell in love with her. He was a
rich militarist, but she listened carefully to his love-
making and did not forget to ask him about the plans to

crush the peasants. He told her—and she sent the news to the peasant army beyond. One of the leaders of this army beyond was her husband.

At last the peasants attacked the city. And so bold had Shan-fei become in her propaganda among the troops that she was arrested and condemned to death. She sent for the official who was in love with her. He listened to her denials, believed them, released her, and enabled her to leave the city. But the peasant army was defeated; among those who emerged alive was her husband, who at last found her in Wuhan.

Shan-fei was next put in charge of the technical work of the party, setting type and printing. She would lay her child on the table by her side and croon to it as she worked. Then one day her home was raided by soldiers. Her husband was away and she had stepped out for a few minutes only. From afar she saw the soldiers guarding her house. Hours later she crept back to find her child. The soldiers had thrown it into a pail of water and left it to die. Not all the tender care of herself and her husband could hold the little thing to life. Shan-fei's husband dried her bitter tears with his face—and Shan-fei turned to her work again.

Some things happen strangely. And one day this happened to Shan-fei; she went to visit the principal of the school where she had once been a student and decided to remain for the night. With the early dawn next morning she was awakened by many shouting voices. She imagined she heard her husband's voice among them. She sat up and listened and heard distinctly the shouts: "We die for the sake of Communism! Long live the Revolution!" Her friend covered her ears with a pillow and exclaimed: "Each day they bring Communists here to shoot or behead them—they are using that open space as an execution ground!"

A series of volleys rang out, and the shouting voices

were silenced. Shan-fei arose and blindly made her way to the execution ground. The soldiers were marching away and only a small crowd of onlookers stood staring stupidly at the long row of dead bodies. Shan-fei stumbled down the line and turned over the warm body of her dead husband.

The net of the White Terror closed in on Shan-fei until she was ordered to leave Wuhan. She went from city to city on the Yangtze, working in factories, organizing women and children. Never could she keep a position for long, because her crippled feet made it impossible for her to stand at a machine for twelve or fourteen hours a day.

In the summer of 1929 she was again with the peasants in Hunan. Sent into Changsha one day, she was captured, together with two men Communists, one a peasant leader. She sat in prison for six months and was released then only because some new militarists over-threw the old, and in revenge freed many prisoners. But they did not free the peasant leader. Shan-fei bribed a prison guard and was permitted to see him before she left. About his neck, his ankles and his wrists were iron bands, and these were connected with iron chains. The life of such prisoners in China is said to be two years. Shan-fei herself had not been chained. But she emerged from prison with a skin disease, with stomach trouble, with an abscess, and her skin was pasty white from anemia. In this condition she returned to the peasantry and took up her fight.

In the spring of 1930 she was sent as a delegate to the All-China Soviet Congress. Friends afterwards put her in a hospital and she was operated on for the abcess. During this period she kept the translation of Marxian studies under her pillow, and she once remarked: "Now I have time to study theory."

There are those who will ask: "Is Shan-fei young and beautiful?"

Shan-fei is twenty-five years of age. Her skin is dark and her face broad; her cheek bones are high. Her eyes are as black as midnight, but they glisten and seem to see through a darkness that is darker than the midnight in China. She is squarely built like a peasant and it seems that it would be very difficult to push her off the earth—so elemental is she, so firmly rooted to the earth. Beautiful? I do not know—is the earth beautiful?

MINING FAMI- LIES

Today I visited the miner Partisans again. I talked with three miners who helped the Eighth Route Army fight the Japanese at Kwangyangchen. One of them told me his story. He was once a soldier in General Feng Yu-hsiang's army, and later became a miner in the Kailin mines at Tangshan, Hopei Province. The Japanese invasion left him unemployed and he found a job in the terrible coal mines at Tatung, North Shansi, where he worked for twenty to thirty cents a day and lived like a dog. When the Communist Party began organizing the men he was arrested and sentenced to twelve years in

China Fights Back, pp. 155-58. This is excerpted from Smedley's diary at Sikwei, Eastern Shansi, November 10, 1937. The writers mentioned toward the end are Hsu Chuen and Chou Li-po. both friends and traveling companions of Smedley. Hsu Chuen, from Manchuria, fell into obscurity. By the late 1940s Chou Li-po had become an important novelist, fulfilling the potential for social realism that Smedley saw in him in novels like *Hurricane*.

the Taiyuan prison. With the Japanese invasion and the building of the national front, he was released and was sent to Yangchüan, on the Chentai railway, to organize the miners there into Partisans. The mines were closed and but two hundred miners remained. He organized them into an armed Partisan group, along with the railway workers there. They blew up the railway as the Japanese advanced; they helped the Eighth Route Army blow up the railroad line at various other places, and finally they fought from November 2nd to 4th at Kwangyangchen (south-west of Yangchüan) and helped the Eighth Route Army score its victory in the afternoon and night of November 4th.

The Partisans have their families with them. Li-po talked with the old mother of one of the men. She is sixty-one years old, grey-haired, strong, militant. She told him that she had two sons, one of whom is a Partisan here and the other a Volunteer. "Do not think of taking care of me," she told them. "Go and fight the enemy. I order you!" She is now with the elder son and is sewing and knitting socks for all the Partisans. She is the mother of the whole group.

As they came down from Yangchüan the miners saw the dead bodies of many slaughtered Chinese youths. In many places the Japanese had taken one, two or three men from each family and killed them; they had sometimes killed all the young men of a village. They roped them together and then split their heads open with swords, on the general theory that living Chinese—particularly youths—are "dangerous." Many people, the miners said, merely watched the Japanese come. But now they have learned a bloody lesson. They know now what the Japanese occupation means—and they are fighting it.

It was difficult to realize, except for the language, that I was talking to Chinese miners, and their wives, sisters and daughters. Some way or other, the miners of all countries look alike, move alike, have the same kind of hands into which coal dust is beaten or rubbed. There is a decision about them, a kind of grim attitude that is still friendly, and an intelligence that arouses respect. Their problems are almost the same, though the problems of the Chinese miners are greater and more difficult than those of Americans. They told of their miserable conditions of life, of their struggle to organize, and of imprisonment and torture. And yet, when the Japanese invasion began, they took up arms to defend their country. They have a great advantage, however, over the oppressed of other countries: they have the Eighth Route Army, an army of workers and peasants, to help them, to train them, to take them into its ranks.

We met groups of armed miners escorting more of their women to the rear. The women might have been the wives or daughters of American or European miners. Like their men, they were grim—perhaps a bit more grim than the men. Their hair was a bit stringy about their faces, they stood firmly on their feet, and they sometimes propped their hands on their hips or folded them across their waists in front of them.

I left the miners feeling once more that I am nothing but a writer, a mere onlooker. I look at their big, black-veined hands, at their cloth shoes worn down to their socks or bare feet, at their soiled shirts. I know there is no chance for me ever to know them and share their lives. I remain a teller of tales, a writer of things through which I have not lived. The real story of China can be told only by the Chinese workers and peasants themselves. To-day that is impossible. I do not believe that my companions, Chinese though they are, can write the real story of the struggle of the Chinese people. They are true Chinese intellectuals, as removed from the life of the masses as I am. And one of them, Hsu Chuen, is first of all interested in "style."

If you ask him about a book, he will tell you first of its style. Later on you can pry out of him something of the content. Li-po is more interested in content, it is true. But the life he lives is so hard now that he is often too weary to make use of his experiences. Later on he will become hardened to this way of life, I think. What I write is not the essence of the Chinese struggle for liberation. It is the record of an observer.

AFTER-WORD

By Florence Howe

Since I had indicated on my customs declaration that I was carrying books as gifts from The Feminist Press to friends and libraries inside the People's Republic of China, a young official at the Peking Airport asked to see them. He could not read English, or so it seemed, for he scanned the several dozen Feminist Press volumes for illustrations alone, raising eyebrows particularly at the pictures in *Witches, Midwives and Nurses* and questioning the drawing of rats on the bedding of a sick woman in *Complaints and Disorders*. Indeed, he seemed to be setting those books aside for further investigation. When he reached into the bottom of the bag to bring out the half-dozen copies of Agnes Smedley's *Daughter of Earth*, I felt less worried: "Smedley," I said, "she was Chu Teh's biographer, and a friend of the People's Republic."

But my pronunciation of "Chu Teh" and "Smedley" made no impression, and so I began to tell the story of Chu Teh's life and Smedley's work in China. Before I had gotten far, the head of a floor-sweeper popped up from behind a tall counter: "Shmedaleya," he said, "Aganessa Shmedaleya," and he continued in Chinese for several lengthy sentences, through which I could occasionally make out the two names in their Chinese pronunciation. Suddenly, all suspicion vanished. The official smiled and offered to help me repack the books scattered along the counter. The questions were now friendly: "You are a teacher?" he asked, grinning broadly. "Yes," I smiled back, "and I teach about Aganessa Shmedaleya."

Daughter of Earth, Smedley's autobiographical and only novel, is not widely known in China. But I tell this story to make clear that Smedley herself is still better known there than in the United States. In China, she is known as an American writer honored especially for her humanitarian work behind the battle lines with the people's armies. For a number of years during the thirties she cared for the sick and wounded personally, raised funds for medical supplies and equipment, and recruited foreign doctors from India and elsewhere. All through the thirties, she continued to report the Chinese revolution and the war against Japan, for German, British, and United States newspapers and magazines. The Chinese valued her devotion to accurate reporting and her willingness to travel with the Red Army, even at high cost to her personal health and safety. Today in China, she is remembered, along with Anna Louise Strong, Norman Bethune, Edgar Snow, and others, as one of many foreign friends of the revolution.

In the United States, twenty-six years after her death, Smedley is beginning to be known as a talented writer of a single work, *Daughter of Earth*, first published in 1929 and rescued from its undeserved obscurity by The

Feminist Press reprint series in 1973. [1] *Daughter of Earth* is fast becoming an important text in American literature courses, as well as in the newer curriculum of courses in autobiography and in women's studies generally. When I remarked that I "teach about Agnes Smedley," I was, of course, thinking about that autobiographical novel, since that has been (apart from her biography of Chu Teh) the only readily available piece of her work.

Portraits of Chinese Women makes "more Smedley" available, both to those who would know more about her and to those who are interested in China. This new volume is an effort to broaden Smedley's reputation as a writer, to indicate the range of her talents and interests, as well as to bring together in one volume most of her writing about Chinese women.

Jan and Steve MacKinnon have written authoritatively about women in Chinese history and about Smedley's life, especially the period in China. From their introduction, one gets a sense of how much of Chinese history and culture Smedley was able—in the parsimonious manner of the good writer—to capture in her stories and sketches. What I want to do is something else: to talk about her work as literature—as writing that is memorable enough to endure, to speak to generations beyond the writer's. I want also to discuss her major themes in this volume and in *Daughter of Earth*, with special attention to feminism.

"Do not make it 'literary' "

At the conclusion of a letter from the battlefront in the late thirties, asking her publisher for assistance, Smedley wrote, "So I beg of you to help me by editing my manuscript—yet do not make it 'literary.' " [2] It is not surprising that the word "literary" was not appealing to her, nor that she disparaged an emphasis on "style" and prefered writers who would talk principally about "content." [3] The reasons for such attitudes are not obscure: as a self-taught writer and intellectual, identifying with many of the political and artistic ideals of the Left of the thirties, Smedley heard in terms like "literary" and "style" both class privilege and irrelevance to the lives of ordinary people. For such terms suggested a world inhabited not by peasants, soldiers, landlords, misery, and war, but rather by the fast living, chic clothes, and cars of Gatsbys. Smedley said of one contemporary Chinese, to whom she compared her own writing, that he is an intellectual "as removed from the life of the masses [in China] as I am"; and of another, Li-Po, who was very much engaged with "the masses," that his life "is so hard now that he is often too weary to make use of his experiences." [4] As a foreign journalist covering a revolution, Smedley knew she was in a unique position. Though her health was often bad, though she worked under conditions of incredible hardship even when her health was reasonably satisfactory, her job demanded that she write and conditions were arranged, even on battlefronts, so that she could.

She was, in short, a working journalist—and, in addition, one who recognized in her work a responsibility beyond getting the story out. As a journalist, her range was very broad. Like the young Kipling, a number of her pieces were written as "stories," though they were originally published in newspapers and news magazines. And, despite her disclaimer about style, she was a careful writer. The variety included in this single volume suggests that, in a sense, she spent the decade in China deliberately experimenting with a number of ways to write, expanding not only her political consciousness but her art. Though we do not yet have access to her papers, which include journals and notebooks, internal evidence alone suggests that she revised and reshaped pieces. [5] Not working to meet daily deadlines, especially after the first few years in China, she had a certain space to revise and reshape as the meaning of events came into focus.

But it is not simply as a good writer that she matters to us today. Nor it it chiefly the unique combination of her circumstances as a writer: an American feminist, a woman with working-class roots living in China during a decade of revolution. The main reason she is so precious to us as a feminist writer today is that she chose to devote her art to the lives of those who do not usually have the time, space, or tools to make their own voices heard. She made a political choice: to remain in China for as long as she could and to put her art on the side of the revolution. She did not have to be inaccurate or untruthful to do this; indeed, the conditions under which old China suffered and new China struggled to be born demanded truth and accurate reporting. But how to tell the story so that it reflected not the glory—or pain—of a few individuals, but of a revolution?

Even in *Daughter of Earth*, which was Smedley's own story, she had tried, as a writer, to deal with the dilemma: Is the protagonist so special as to rise above her social class? Marie Rogers, her protagonist self, is a strong, romantic individual. She suffers, but she succeeds in freeing herself from the lives her mother, sister, and aunt lived. Still, she speaks early in the novel of belonging to "those who do not die for the sake of beauty":

> I belong to those who die from other causes—exhausted by poverty, victims of wealth and power, fighters in a great cause. A few of us die, desperate from the pain or disillusionment of love, but for most of us "the earthquake but discloseth new fountains." For

we are of the earth and our struggle is the struggle of earth. [6]

Smedley's problem throughout that novel is how to make it clear that though Marie Rogers *is* distinctive and escapes being crushed by the conditions faced by working-class women, she does not, in fact, leave the others behind her, in the manner of the conventional second generation of succeeders in the United States. She does not scorn her parents, her sister and brothers, and her prostitute aunt. She gives voice to their suffering and deprivations: the vision of their lives is always before her.

During the last years of her life in the United States at the end of the forties, Smedley was working on a biography of the peasant general, Chu Teh. The book was published posthumously, though, as the publisher wrote, it was "all in first draft which she intended to revise as well as supplement." [7] Whether she would have changed her style we will never know. As it was written, Smedley's method as a biographer included her own presence, and as the following makes clear, her own presence means also her ancestral or class consciousness. Chu Teh is speaking, having already told her that he looks like his mother, who had borne thirteen children, the last five of whom "were drowned at birth because we were too poor to feed so many mouths."

"It did not matter to the landlord that the peasants did not have enough food for themselves, or that they were needed at home for plowing or harvesting," General Chu remarked bitterly. "The men of my family had to go, and my mother or foster mother had to work in the King of Hell's kitchen. When they returned home they sometimes brought out some choice bit of food which they had hidden in their clothing, and gave us children each a bite; and they told us tales that sounded like fairy stories."

Sometimes, when General Chu talked like this, I would be unable to go on and he would regard me with curious and questioning eyes.

"Sometimes," I would explain, "you seem to be describing my own mother. We did not work for a feudal landlord, but my mother washed clothing for rich people and worked in their kitchens during holidays. She would sometimes sneak out food for us children, give us each a bite, and tell us of the fine food in the home of her employer. Her hands, too, were almost black from work, and she wore her hair in a knot at the nape of her neck. Her hair was black and disheveled."

"And your father?" he asked in wonderment.

"In my early childhood he was a poor farmer who plowed the fields in his bare feet, but wore leather shoes most of the time. He ran away periodically because he hated our life, and left my mother alone. He was not so disciplined as the men of your family. Then he became an unskilled day laborer, and we never had enough to eat. But we did have salt enough."

"The poor of the world are one big family," he said in his hoarse voice, and we sat for a long time in silence. [8]

Smedley's interviews with Chu Teh took place at or near the front during the mid-thirties. She wants to tell the story of his life, she tells Chu Teh, "because you are a peasant. Eight out of every ten living Chinese are peasants. Not one has ever told his story to the world. If you would tell me your life story, a peasant would be speaking for the first time." She continues, characteristically, "I . . . met many men of more dramatic charac-

ter than General Chu, men whose lives are the stuff
from which great literature is made. Chinese peasants,
however, are not dramatic, and I clung to my original
idea. . . ." [9] The stories written during all her years in
China give every evidence of a similar consciousness and
of a similar effort to work out the writer's problem:
How to individualize and yet generalize at the same
time? How to make the story as real as its particularity
and yet extend its implications not only to other
individuals, but beyond individuality? How to write
with the factual truth of "journalism" and yet produce
writing that will live beyond its first appearance?

In "Five Women of Mukden" and in "Hsu Mei-ling"
she tries two different approaches. "Five Women"
sketches women in northern Manchuria across a range of
ages and classes in 1930. The devoted wife raising
money for a politically imprisoned husband, the teacher
who is allowed to visit women imprisoned for murdering
their husbands, the cursing sprawled peasant and her
tiny child, the old-fashioned wife, and the devoted
mother and student daughter—each figure or grouping is
used to tell a bit of social history, not only of individuals but of groups. The slightest of these, for example,
the picture of the mother and daughter on the tramway,
catches in two brief paragraphs the "many decades of
culture" separating Chinese generations, and the results
of that gulf: increased hostility between older men and
the new generation of male students (and revolutionaries); continued hostility between older men and new
women students; and the solidarity between women and
men students, as well as their understanding of the
subjection of women in China.

In "Hsu Mei-ling" Smedley tries a very different
method, one that we may recognize as more "literary"
or at least more like short stories we are accustomed to.
That is, the main character has a name and a specific

rather than a generic problem. She has weaknesses and
strengths and is engaged in a slight plot, an attempt to
win her husband away from his "affair with the white-
guard Russian dancing girl." Her husband, too, is speci-
fied as a man in love with modernism, "which he
confuses with Americanism." They have young daughters, including an eight-year-old who can dance the
Charleston. Mei-ling's husband doesn't want to bring the
Russian dancer home; he wants, in a more modern
fashion, "to put away"—or divorce—his wife.

Smedley's feminist eye is interested in the struggle
inside Mei-ling, to whose character she is both drawn
and repulsed: "Her whole being breathes the reserve, the
dignity and the composure of the old-fashioned girl. But
she is also ignorant, superstitious and suspicious, and
understands only one relationship between men and
women." Despite that servile relationship, Mei-ling re-
fuses to attend American films with her husband several
times each week: she cannot bear the nakedness of the
women and their open sexuality. It is, in its own way,
an heroic gesture that Smedley, for her own reasons,
admires, as she does Mei-ling's determination to observe
first-hand her husband's new love dancing. But the end
is both pathetic and painfully comic, as Mei-ling begs
Smedley to teach *her* to dance and, after "a few lame
steps" on her once bound, then unbound but crippled
feet, stands weeping while the phonograph yelps its
modern song of love.

It is Hsu Mei-ling's troubled story, yet Smedley also
sketches her husband, who manages to combine the
feudalism of China that insists upon the oppression of
wives with the modernism of the West that allows a
more open form of sexuality as veneer for the general
oppression of women. It is a sketch, moreover, pro-
jected economically onto a broader screen of China in
transition, for the husband is an Americanized bank

clerk with ambitions of becoming an executive for the Ford Motor Company's interests in China.

In "Five Women" there is also a sketch of an old-fashioned wife. But she is more sparingly drawn as "old, worn out and ugly," albeit with "intelligent" eyes. Her drama is not her own, for she "does not dare object" to her husband's desire to "buy a sing-song girl of sixteen and bring her home as his second wife." The conflict focuses on the father and his eldest son, who is his mother's protector. The point for Smedley is not only the oppression of wives, but the conflict between generations, arising out of the new revolutionary consciousness in which feminism is a significant ingredient. [10]

"Five Women" is no less memorable for its style than "Hsu Mei-ling"; they represent two different efforts, polarized here as the generic and the individualistic modes. They serve different political and aesthetic functions. Smedley found other literary ways to approach her political mission, but before turning to these, it may be illuminating to write briefly about the person who became her literary and, in certain respects, political mentor in China.

"I am tortured always by this inequality"

Smedley was fortunate enough to have gone to China in time to know Lu Hsun during his last half-dozen years. Described generally as the father of modern Chinese literature, Lu Hsun was also a self-taught writer who had begun by studying medicine in Japan, but who had turned to literature as a strategy for effecting changes in the minds and hearts of his compatriots. By the time Smedley came to know him, he was both a political activist and the author of three volumes of short stories, now classics, written mainly during the years from 1919 to 1926. Smedley helped to translate some of these stories, lived with his family, and worked with Lu Hsun on several other literary projects. It would be surprising had he not, therefore, affected her work and her conception of herself as a writer.

At first glance, the volume of Lu Hsun's stories, published in English translation by China's Foreign Language Press, seems comparable to Smedley's *Portraits of Chinese Women in Revolution* in only one major respect: both Lu Hsun and Smedley are "tortured always by . . . inequality." [11] While Lu Hsun's stories chronicle the lives of a broad range of Chinese people, from the most impoverished and suffering to the most carelessly rich, the focus is on the unfortunate, usually helpless, victim. There is little hope in most of the stories, few signs of a struggle for change, and only glimmers of consciousness from an occasional narrator or character. What comes through is the incredible endurance of people despite the most wretched of conditions, the most barbaric of beliefs, and even, on the part of some, the most impervious cruelty to others. The mute martyrs gleam memorably, though they are never heroic figures. Taken together, Lu Hsun's stories cry out for something to be done: that "something" itself is signified only in tiny details, as in the story called "An Incident."

Barely two and one-half pages, "An Incident" is the story of a rickshaw driver who abandons his client to rescue a poor, old woman. The passenger/narrator at first resents the rickshaw man's concern, feels that the old woman "must be pretending," and that the rickshaw driver will get what he deserves if the woman chooses to fill out a complaint against him in the police station. Abandoned, the narrator has no choice but to sit a silent witness to the scene:

Suddenly I had a strange feeling. His dusty, retreating figure seemed larger at that instant. Indeed, the further he walked the larger he loomed, until I had to look up to him. At the same time he seemed gradually to be exerting a pressure on me, which threatened to overpower the small self under my fur-lined gown.

My vitality seemed sapped as I sat there motionless, my mind a blank, until a policeman came out.

The policeman tells the narrator to "Get another rickshaw. He can't pull you any more." "Without thinking," the narrator says, "I pulled a handful of coppers from my coat pocket and handed them to the policeman." The narrator asks that they be given to the driver. Over the years, the narrator tells us, the incident "keeps coming back to me, often more vivid than in actual life, teaching me shame, urging me to reform, and giving me fresh courage and hope." [1 2]

It *is* a tiny incident. We in the West might easily pass right over it, the detail of the narrator's "fur-lined gown" hardly noticeable against the detail of the old woman's "tattered jacket, unbuttoned and fluttering in the wind"—that catches in the rickshaw and makes her fall. We are also not accustomed to the scene: a person harnessed to draw another person in comfort. What gives the "misanthropic" narrator, writing in 1920 about an incident that occurred in the winter of 1917, "courage and hope"? As one learns from the rest of the stories in Lu Hsun's volume, bold solidarity among the poor and the oppressed is not a common occurrence in old China.

Nor could Lu Hsun's stories, written in the early twenties, celebrate the heroism of revolutionaries, or of intellectuals like himself. In the preface to his first collection, he describes a "feeling of loneliness ... coiling about my soul like a huge poisonous snake." [1 3]

His escape from this loneliness was to write. And while he wrote mainly of the sufferings of old China, and out of his own personal pessimism, he admitted also that he "could not blot out hope, for hope lies in the future." [14]

The extent to which Smedley's approach to the issue of the political functions of the writer was shaped by her association with Lu Hsun cannot yet be stated with certainty. Like other students of Lu Hsun, a generation or more younger than the master, she took a more directly active role in political and military events than he had. And unlike the Lu Hsun of the late teens and early twenties, she had a much more clearly active political movement about which to write and with which to identify. Lu Hsun could only suggest glimmers of a changed future—for there were then only glimmers, even with the emergence of the May Fourth Movement. Fifteen years later, the Chinese Communist Party had succeeded in establishing zones of control and the long-term revolutionary struggle had begun in earnest. Events thus made it possible for Smedley to place "courage and hope" squarely in the middle of her canvas.

It is not only class or female solidarity that she celebrates—in a few instances with joy and humor, as among the peasant women led by Mother Tsai in "The Women Take a Hand" or among the "Silk Workers" in Kwangtung. It is also open conflict inside families, between generations, between husbands and wives, and especially across class lines. Even when the conflict occurs within class lines, as in "A White Episode," and the story is of unmitigated horror and cruelty inflicted by poor Chinese soldiers against Chinese peasants, the net effect is not total despair. For the story turns delicately on literacy and illiteracy, rather than on the martyrdom of the young pregnant woman and the

younger boy. Their heroism depends on their "knowing," as the villainy of their compatriots depends on
their being kept in feudal ignorance. In this story,
perhaps more than in any other in the volume, Smedley
accomplishes what Lu Hsun does with apparent ease
again and again. The characters are drawn in bold brush
strokes in which individuality never clouds their generic
raison d'être.

In styles used also by Lu Hsun, Smedley attempts, in
two more ambitious stories, to write the histories of
privileged women who crossed class lines in China to
join the revolution. In "Shan-fei, Communist" and "The
Dedicated" Smedley is not simply telling her Western
audience that women's lives are changing somewhat. She
is frankly promoting the fact that women have taken a
bold hand in changing their lives in order to effect
revolutionary changes in all people's lives. She is, in
short, attempting to write, within the framework of
accurate history of two women's lives, the generic
history of revolutionary Chinese feminists.

It is a difficult assignment, and Smedley adopts styles
that are unfamiliar to her. They are also not what
Western readers are accustomed to. They do not focus
sufficiently on "scenes"; they contain virtually no dia-
logue; their view is generic not individualistic; their
ideology is explicit—all of which we do not expect from
fiction or reportage.

Not surprisingly, the results are mixed. If we are
looking for individual idiosyncrasies in characterization
and an emphasis on personal relations, we shall be
disappointed. If we are interested in history and moved
by social documentary, we will consider Smedley's
efforts worthwhile, if flawed. These stories may also
help to answer questions that Western feminists like
myself have put to the Chinese, partly out of their own
ignorance of Chinese history and ideology, partly out of

their own confusion about the relationship between class and feminism.

Both stories are, at least to begin with, stories of women's liberation. In each case, a woman is helped by other women to free herself from feudal family ties and beliefs to become a leading Communist. Their chronicles cover a similar span of years, with similar attention to the brief spasms of successful revolution, then counter-revolution, in the late twenties. Both marry, beneath their social class, peasant men who die young as revolutionaries. But the two women and their stories are quite different, despite what I have called a generic rather than an individualistic approach to characterization. And, indeed, Shan-fei, in the briefer treatment and despite an incredible series of narrow escapes, emerges as a more believable person than Chang Siao-hung (of "The Dedicated"), perhaps because, unlike Chang Siao-hung, she does not tell her own story.

In each case, Smedley chronicles roughly the same period of time that occupies *Daughter of Earth*—much of the first three decades of a woman's life, and much of that the first three decades of the twentieth century. In the case of "Shan-fei, Communist," Smedley experiments with the third person and the spare "outline" form of traditional Chinese story-telling for which Lu Hsun is acclaimed. Smedley tersely narrates the facts of Shan-fei's life, with two distinct ideological emphases. First she concerns herself with the liberation of women, through the "pioneering" efforts of Shan-fei's foot-bound mother, who, learning from her student son, fights "the enemy"—her husband and his brother—for her daughter's education and eventual freedom. The second half is the story of a revolutionary woman. The narrative allows only a sentence for the birth of her child, only several more for the child's cruel death at the hands of soldiers, no space to Shan-fei's life with her

peasant husband, two paragraphs to his death, less than
that to her six-month imprisonment. Rather, these
events fold into her work as a revolutionary, among
peasants, in factories, as head of the Woman's Department of the Kuomintang, as spy and propagandist.
Frankly ideological, the story's concluding message is
offered in terms that remind us of the story's feminist
theme and of Smedley's own class-conscious *Daughter
of Earth*:

> There are those who will ask: "Is Shan-fei young and
> beautiful?"
> . . . She is squarely built like a peasant and it seems
> that it would be very difficult to push her off the
> earth—so elemental is she, so firmly rooted to the
> earth. Beautiful? I do not know—is the earth beautiful?

"The Dedicated" is more moving as social history and
less successful as fiction than "Shan-fei, Communist." It
is not easy to write about revolutionaries. One can too
readily fall into the traps of glorification or vilification.
Smedley briefly glorifies Chang Siao-hung as she intro-
duces her appearance on "the great historical stage."
Her face is "of inspired intelligence," her eyes "see
everything, understand everything." She is to speak in
the unbroken monologue adopted from "the old feudal
stage of China," on which "actors . . . often step
forward to explain what rôle they are playing." The
style of Smedley's introduction is unusually lyrical,
perhaps deliberately to contrast with Chang Siao-hung's
factual opening voice. Her monologue, it is soon apparent, allows for two kinds of motion forward into the
story: the narrative of her life, prefaced first by the life
of her grandfather, and in general, a low-keyed outline;
and lengthy digressions, sometimes with rhetorical and
analytical flourishes on such social evils as the slave

trade in the daughters of poor peasants. The story's pace is slower than "Shan-fei, Communist," its fabric the detail of social history, political analysis, and reportage. The feminist theme is more complexly rooted here in China's revolution.

Born into poverty, Siao-hung's grandfather seizes an opportunity offered by the British in Hong Kong, and in his lifetime rises to lavish new wealth on his family, who become participants in the exploitation of others. Imperialist wealth also brings with it certain progressive ideas, including the education of women. At the same time that Siao-hung becomes the first girl to attend a daring new coeducational school in Hong Kong, she is also witness to her grandmother's kitchen sale of poor, peasant girls. The child's experience, reminiscent of the Grimké sisters', provides Siao-hung with the formal motivation for her life-long sense of outrage at injustice. A further lengthy digression, to describe contract labor, a contemporary form of "the trade in men slaves," serves both to extend the analysis of imperialism's effects on China's feudalism and also to underscore the fact that the oppression of women is but one half of the problem. When Siao-hung returns to the outline of her privileged life, it is framed by what she calls "this story of human slavery ... one of the countless facts of human subjection that awakened me to my duty, that showed me the face of the ruling class."

Of course it is her face too, until she separates herself from it. Her sisters, both of whom are unhappily married, help in her struggles with her family. Not only does she avoid marriage on their terms; she gains an education as a physician, determined to "serve the workers and peasants of China." Again, the monologue moves between the narrative of the individual woman, describing her years of study, her membership in the Communist party, her "strong and tough" body at work on the battlefield, where tears were replaced by "iron" conviction and "energy"; and the more brilliant depiction of horrors, first of the Peking massacre of March 18, 1926, and then of the Canton massacre of 1927. Smedley does not flinch before barbarism. For Siao-hung, it is a final reminder of the class she was born to, and even the gender, for she describes how "bourgeois women go through the streets, bend over wounded and dying workingmen, and beat out their brains with chunks of stone or wood"—and worse.

The story concludes with Siao-hung's rhetorical peroration as a Communist: all that she has learned "as a member of the privileged classes I have now placed at the disposal of the peasants and the workers." Indeed, her individuality is irrelevant: she is truly part of historical events, of an ongoing revolution.

If both of these stories—"Shan-fei, Communist" and "The Dedicated"—are not, in our usual terms, successful fiction, it may be that we ask of them what Smedley will not—or cannot—provide: the dailiness of personal life for revolutionary women who must live, like male Chinese revolutionaries, without familial ties, without sexuality, without the love of husband or children. What Smedley provides, instead, is a glimpse into motivation: for Shan-fei, the "rebellious," "strange" mother; for Siao-hung, the grandmother's avarice and the girl slaves' tears. What Smedley provides in far larger measure are social history and ideology, woven into narrative or monologue, in an attempt to explain to a Western audience the inextricable link between the liberation of Chinese women and the Communist revolution. The emphasis on class again supports the effort to write generic not individualistic histories.

For Smedley also, these stories are part of an effort to solve the problem of being a political writer, to discover a style in which she can be writer and partisan, rather than, as she usually puts it, "nothing but a writer, a mere onlooker." [15] These pieces, like others included in this volume from *Chinese Destinies*, are relatively early efforts to use her journalist's ear and eye and her knowledge of historical events in the making of stories.

"I hungered for the spark of vision"

The political function of the writer was, for Smedley, not an abstract question. In addition to the matter of nationality—she was an American, not a Chinese—which continued to nag her, there was the daily issue of the writer's priorities. In *Battle Hymn of China*, for example, she describes how, at the start of the Sino-Japanese War, in the summer of 1937, "Chu Teh started for the front and I was left with another unfinished book. . . . I asked Mao Tze-tung," she continues,

> which he thought more important for me to do—remain in Yenan and write Chu Teh's biography, or go to the front and write of the war.
> Mao Tze-tung said: "This war is more important than past history."
> So I stored my notebooks and prepared to go to the front. [16]

From that front, Smedley sent back the dispatches that make up *China Fights Back*, a volume that deserves reprinting for its immediate record of a war and for the view of Smedley as working journalist.

"Mining Families," the last piece in this volume, comes from *China Fights Back*. It records an instance of Smedley's inability to forget her own American past: "the miners of all countries," she tells us, "look alike. . . ." But despite the reminder that she, too, had a

father and a mother who resembled these Chinese
mining families, for Smedley the incident serves to
emphasize her distance from that past and from the
present lives of the Chinese as well—for she is a writer:

> I left the miners feeling once more that I am nothing
> but a writer, a mere onlooker. I look at their big,
> black-veined hands, at their cloth shoes worn down to
> their socks or bare feet, at their soiled shirts. I know
> there is no chance for me ever to know them and
> share their lives. I remain a teller of tales, a writer of
> things through which I have not lived.

Finally, she concludes, "What I write is not the essence
of the Chinese struggle for liberation. It is the record of
an observer."

Elsewhere in *China Fights Back*, where Smedley
draws a similar distinction between her privileges and
the deprivations of Chinese soldiers, she makes even
clearer her apprehension that her status as foreign
"onlooker" interferes with her goals as a writer. "The
real story of China," Smedley insists, "can be told only
by the Chinese workers and peasants themselves." If
"to-day that is impossible,"[17] if she is the only person
available at the moment, so be it. As writer, she is not
miner, soldier, worker, peasant—American or Chinese.
Thus, she must continue to hunger "for the spark of
vision that would enable me to see into their minds and
hearts. . . ."[18]

But that is not the only tension. There is also the
traditional one—can she be partisan and still write "a
very fine book"? Towards the end of *Battle Hymn of
China*—in my view one of the best books ever written on
China—she comes at this question directly:

> Jack Belden carried a copy of Tolstoy's *War and
> Peace* with him and said that if the names and places

were changed into Chinese, it might easily seem like a version of the present war. He asked me who could write such a book on China and I said that I thought it could be done only by a Chinese who had actually fought throughout the whole of it. But I also thought that Jack might one day write a very fine book. He had been with many Chinese armies and in order to reach them had had to use all kinds of maneuvers to get past officials. He was more objective than I; he represented no cause and could stand aside and observe, whereas I always forgot that I was not a Chinese myself. To me the problems, strength and weaknesses of China seemed to be those of the whole world. [19]

It is not false modesty that makes Smedley minimize her own destiny, nor can one blame her self-denials either on personal feelings of inferiority or on ideological conviction about the appropriate self-effacing stance of writers. She is wrestling with difficult literary and political questions, and those of us who write and read will, of necessity, also continue to wrestle with them.

In *Battle Hymn of China*, Smedley resolves some of these tensions in practice. Several of the pieces from *Battle Hymn* included here are, in my opinion, among Smedley's best work. In "Silk Workers," for example, Smedley is the working journalist whose story illuminates the special ability of an onlooker to peel away the layers of official misinformation to get at the truth about women, work, and feminism in Kwangtung. In "The Women Take a Hand," Smedley is a hospital worker who is known as a feminist. Thus, she is naturally privy to the local organizing of peasant women and to their struggles against an opium merchant. She is an observer who can cheer from the sidelines, as she tells a good story of heroic women. In "Chinese Patricians,"

my favorite piece, Smedley offers another self-portrait
and, at the same time, a more panoramic view of the
Chinese scene.

The immediate theme is death, and, by contrast, the
richness of life, especially as illustrated by the ritual of a
Chinese feast. The ultimate question is, as in Lu Hsun's
"An Incident," "What is to be done"? The method of
the piece is contrast. Smedley's friends, "Chinese Patricians," are male "modern" intellectual pragmatists who
scorn physical labor and politics, refuse to believe in the
reality of classes in China, and still follow feudal
practices with regard to women. The feminist Smedley
is an anomaly: "To them I was not man, woman,
concubine, or courtesan. I was a foreigner who was no
longer young, was not beautiful, earned her own living,
and associated with men as an equal. Neither wifehood
nor love was my profession." She is, she need not say it
openly, a writer. She is also, with them, openly partisan
about feminism and about the Chinese revolution.

From a description of one of the patrician's work as
an archaeologist in the vicinity of the Yellow River,
Smedley moves rapidly to consider the river's contemporary scene—war, famine, floods; to describe a visit to
a match factory in which the workers are small children
who rarely outlive their childhood; to name in rapid
succession the causes of deaths of the miserable poor
and the fearful rich; and finally to challenge the patricians with the vision of poor students who "braved"
death "and thought only in terms of the social revolution."

The feast follows, its conviviality seeming to eradicate
all conflicts "about Chinese women and patricians and
proletarians." But the ending, riding "home in rickshas
through the cold white streets," shifts into the final
contrast, as Smedley thinks "about my ricksha coolie
silently running like a tired horse before me, his heavy

breath interrupted by a rotten cough. . . . Suddenly," she continues, "his broad shoulders began to remind me of my father's. I was a dog and the whole lot of us were dogs!"

If we are reminded of Lu Hsun's rickshaw story, I think it is no accident. But Smedley, unlike Lu Hsun's narrator, does not sit and think:

> "Listen, you!" I screamed at my hosts in most un-patrician tones. "Get out and pull your ricksha coolie home! Let's all get out and pull our ricksha coolies home! Let's prove there are no classes in China!"

It is an absurd but appropriate conclusion, the proletarian Smedley mocking her activist proclivities by calling for an immediate demonstration of the evening's fraternal fantasies. Here, in effect, she is able to make bold comedy of her dilemma, as well as rich social commentary.

In *Battle Hymn* as a whole, Smedley resolves, or at least holds in creative tension, her literary and political dilemmas. Perhaps she had, by the early forties, gained more confidence about the significance of the writing she had been doing, and that she was to do most forcefully in this book: carrying out the injunction of an heroic, slain Chinese officer who had told her, "We have our faith . . . tell your countrymen. . . ." [20] Perhaps she had found her *métier* in *Battle Hymn's* distinctive blend of autobiography, reportage, portraiture, history, travel narrative, and Tolstoian panorama of a country-side at war. Or perhaps back in the United States, she had the opportunity, forced upon her by ill-health, the spread of the war, and the changing political alignments, to recollect the events of the thirties in a kind of tranquillity unavailable on Chinese soil. Or perhaps it was simply, as she wrote, that "I had become a part of the vast struggle of China." [21] In any event, few books blend so well what I have called the individual with the generic. For the book chronicles Smedley's own journey into the heart of China's revolution and the discovery there of a future in which peasants could not only survive but live in dignity and with hope. Few books succeed as well in creating that sense of courage and hope in the face of what was, especially for Westerners, a war of almost legendary barbarism. *Battle Hymn* ends in 1941, with that war broadening, the revolution unfinished, and Smedley's own life in limbo. It leaves us with a sense of the jagged inconclusiveness of lives that a cosmetic art only blurs.

That *Battle Hymn of China* is still out of print, despite renewed American interest in China, reflects the narrowness of our literary standards. That book, like this new collection, falls into none of the usual categories. Both are the literature of social documentary— and unabashedly partisan. Feminism has helped show many of us the need for fresh categories, for partisan engagement. In these recognitions, perhaps Agnes Smedley can once more serve to teach us.

Notes

I wish to thank Paul Lauter without whom this afterword could not have been written. His vision and intelligence are known; his quiet hard work in the background may not be.

1. *Daughter of Earth* is an autobiographical novel about the first three decades of a working-class woman's life. Tillie Olsen, associated with The Feminist Press from its beginning, suggested that *Daughter* merited reprinting, and Paul Lauter provided a scholarly, biographical afterword. The book introduced Smedley to a modern American audience that, in three years, has grown to a substantial size. The book is in its fifth reprinting; over 30,000 copies have been sold.

2. *China Fights Back* (New York: The Vanguard Press, 1938), p. xvii.

3. "Mining Families," p. 165.

4. *Ibid.*

5. Smedley left her literary remains to Chu Teh, and after her death, they were, with her ashes, flown to China. They have not yet been catalogued and made available to the public.

6. *Daughter of Earth*, p. 8.

7. *The Great Road: The Life and Times of Chu Teh* (New York: Monthly Review Press, 1956), p. xi.

8. *Ibid.*, p. 12, p. 18

9. *Ibid.*, p. 3.

10. The sketch also provides the germ of "The Story of Kwei Chu."

11. *China Fights Back*, p. 18.

12. *Selected Stories of Lu Hsun* (Peking: Foreign Languages Press, 1963), pp. 65-67.

13. *Ibid.*, p. 23.

14. *Ibid.*, p. 24.

15. "Mining Families," p. 164.

16. *Battle Hymn of China* (New York: Alfred A. Knopf, 1943), p. 168.

17. "Mining Families," p. 164.

18. *China Fights Back*, p. 112.

19. *Battle Hymn of China*, pp. 505-6.

20. *Ibid.*, p. 411.

21. *Ibid.*, p. 525.

PHOTO-GRAPHIC POR-TRAITS

Except for the photo on page 194 which includes Smedley herself, the photographs on the following pages are Agnes Smedley's own snapshots of Chinese women taken in the years 1939 and 1940 and are being published here for the first time. Smedley was the only Western journalist who lived for a number of years with Communist-led Chinese troops during World War II. Besides her writing, she left an extensive photographic record of her experiences with the guerrilla troops, the New Fourth Army in particular. After Smedley's death in 1950, her photographs were carefully perserved by her good friend, Toni Willison, and are housed today in the University Archives of Arizona State University, with copies in the People's Revolutionary Museum, Peking. The portrait at left, of Smedley herself, was taken in 1939 by Aino Taylor.   —*The Editors*

*Smedley with
the Women's
Committee
of the
Fifth War Zone,
Hupei*

*The Women's
Corps,
Suchen*

*New Fourth
Army
women nurses*

*Women nurses
with guerrilla
troops
along the
Tientsin-Nanking
Railroad in
Anhui Province*

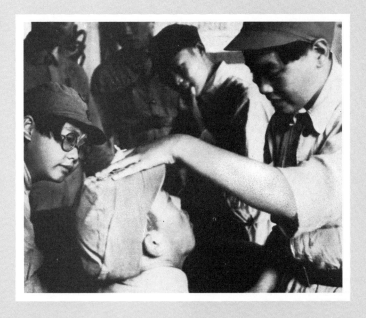

*A meeting
at the Women's
Conference
north of Hankow*

Delegates
to the Women's
Conference
north of Hankow

At right, Miss Li,
Army Medical
Director of
the New
Fourth Army
Storm Guerrilla
Detachment
north of Hankow

*Some leaders
of the
New Fourth Army
Storm Guerrilla
Detachment;
at front left,
Chen Ta-ji,
the top woman
commander*

Some delegates
to the
first conference
of Hsien
in central Hupeh

*Guerrilla
leaders
responsible for
organizing
and educating
civilian women*